"I met Dave Martin for the first time when we were seated together on the same flight. We introduced ourselves and have been friends for over twenty years. The one thing that impressed me at our first meeting and to this day about Dave Martin is how he thinks and can capsulize those thoughts and articulate them for the benefit of others. That's precisely the intent of his latest book, *Mindset Matters*. No doubt, you will read, learn, and shift to your next level."

—SAM CHAND, Leadership Consultant,
Author, and Friend of Dave Martin

"Dr. Dave Martin always knocks it out of the park. He is not only a great speaker but a great leader. I strongly recommend him to any CEO or organization wanting to vigorously move the ball forward with real solutions."

—JACK OWOC
Founder/CEO of Bang Energy

"Dave Martin's teaching has transformed not only me but also my family and business life. I appreciate his wisdom and incredible sense of humor. He captures your attention and allows you to create a new crease in your brain in regards to leadership."

—GILLIAN ORTEGA
Mary Kay, Inc.

"Dr. Dave is one of the most gifted communicators I have ever encountered! A lot of people see how funny he is and recognize the richness of his voice, but beneath the surface is so much substance and insight! It is a privilege to be his friend."

—STEVEN FURTICK
Best-Selling Author and Lead Pastor, Elevation Church

For foreign and subsidiary rights, contact the author.

Cover design by: Joe De Leon
Cover Photo by: Andrew van Tilborgh

ISBN: 978-1-954089-25-9   1 2 3 4 5 6 7 8 9 10

Printed in the United States of America

MINDSET
MATTERS

Change Your Mind   *Change Your World*

DR. DAVE MARTIN

AVAIL

CONTENTS

INTRODUCTION

THE INFLUENCES THAT HAVE
SHAPED MY THINKING

Some people consider me to be a coach—others a pastor. Some esteem me as a mentor—others a teacher. Regardless of the title I use for myself or the labels that others assign to me, my only real goals in life are to become the man God created me to be and help others become the men and women that God created them to be. My definition of success, therefore, is derived from these goals.

For some people, success can only be achieved when they *have* more, *do* more, or *achieve* more than the people who surround them. I see success as something less selfish. Others don't have to fail in order for me to flourish because the standard I am pursuing for my life is not attained when others fall short of theirs; it is only attained when

I know that I have lived up to my own expectations and when the people I serve have lived up to theirs.

Consequently, I try to avoid comparing myself to others. First of all, I am not pursuing the same goals as the people I know. I have different talents. Some of my friends and acquaintances have higher IQs than I do, but I have skills that they don't have. In addition, my friends and I don't share the same dreams, experiences, responsibilities, or circumstances in life—all of which have defined our individual goals and the unique paths we have chosen to reach them.

These reasons are why it would be foolish for me to compare myself to my neighbor. My neighbor's highest and best expectations for his life may be to create a successful business, build a healthy family, or help solve a perplexing social problem like homelessness or illiteracy. My highest and best expectations are the ones that I stated previously: become the man that God has destined me to be and make myself available to help others be the same.

Disregard what drives and inspires you and all the influences that have shaped and helped to define you, and there is one thing that you and I (and everyone else) have in common. We have been heavily influenced and distinctly defined by the voices, experiences, and cultures that have wrought our perspectives, expectations, and pursuits.

That is true of me, you, and everyone living in a free nation where personal choice and individual responsibility are part of the fabric of our lives. I have been shaped by those who came before me, and I am still being shaped by the people I allow to speak into my life directly or through various forms of media—my parents, close friends, teachers, coaches, pastors, and people I have never even met, yet who have inspired me through their achievements or their eloquent words. I continue to be shaped by people with whom I work or encounter in my work and daily life. I travel globally and labor alongside some of the world's most prolific leaders in business, government, faith, and philanthropy. I constantly read books by people who stir me with their unconventional wisdom or their unimaginable achievements.

As time passes and the years of my life accumulate, I see more clearly how all these "influencers" have helped to mold me and set me on the course that I have chosen to walk. One such "influencer" made a particularly strong impression on me. When I was much younger, eager to find and pursue my own personal destiny, I was introduced to one of America's original motivational speakers, Earl Nightingale. I remember hearing his distinctive voice and being amazed by his astounding insights into human character and behavior.

It's been years since I have heard that strong, authoritative voice pierce the airwaves of American radio, but I can still clearly remember some of the astute and stirring things he said. Although Nightingale was not the only person who fed my passion for helping people succeed in life, he was certainly one of the first. So I have come to understand, in a very humbling way, that the person I have become and the things I have been able to achieve are, in part, the result of the wisdom, passion, and insight that Nightingale and all the rest of my "influencers" have poured into me.

Although I cannot recall all the details of his many lectures, I can recall recurring themes Earl Nightingale shared with the public during his pioneering career. Many are rooted in Scripture. Having grown up in a Christian home, where the Word of God was believed and taught, I noticed the evident thread of biblical truth.

For instance, Nightingale frequently used the word "seeds" to illustrate his key points. Jesus did this as well. I remember well his strong insistence that a person's behaviors flow from his choices and that his choices flow from his thinking, another theme that is evident in the teachings of Christ. The concept with which I launch this book—that only about 4 percent of the American population will ever become successful and self-sufficient—I first heard from Earl Nightingale. Although I heard it decades ago, it is a mathematical statistic that I have verified as still being fairly accurate.

Therefore, the material that follows, the ideas that I share in the pages ahead are principles that I gleaned from Earl Nightingale, other great teachers and motivators, the pages of Scripture, and those many attention-grabbing experiences that have opened my eyes to truth. It is the outgrowth of the wisdom that I have gleaned from many sources over many years, wisdom that I better understand at this point in my life because I have had the opportunity to put it into practice and to observe its effectiveness.

I've become the person that I am today because of all the stimuli that have influenced me: words of key and timely influencers, examples, both good and bad, that the authority figures in my life set before my watching eyes, personal experiences, both the pleasant and the painful, and the consequences I have received as a result of my own choices and resulting actions!

I have also become the person I am today because of the choices I have made regarding how I would respond to those stimuli. Where I have made good choices, I have prospered, and where I have made foolish choices, I have suffered. I have learned and grown as a human being through all my decisions, and that is the best that I can expect from myself. That is the best that you can expect from yourself—to learn and to grow through life's pleasant and victorious chapters as well as the torturous and disheartening ones.

As I explained in my opening statement, people tend to call me different things. They describe my work using different labels. One label that is definitely accurate is "coach." I work hard to tell people and to show them through my own life how to succeed in all the important aspects of life. And, remember, I am the product of the wise people who coached me. In the eight chapters that follow, I want to share with you some of the principles and truths that were imparted to me by others and derived from life's experiences, so you can learn, as I learned earlier in my life, to mind your own head. Manage your thinking and the attitudes and actions that flow from it, so you can control your own destiny.

I appreciate all the people who helped shape my thinking when I was younger and highly impressionable. I appreciate my parents, several amazing teachers, a number of pastors who have forever impacted my life, and many of my peers and people from previous generations who shared common-sense wisdom with me. I also appreciate the "voices" of writers, thinkers, and public speakers like Earl Nightingale who have helped me see beyond the limitations of my present circumstances and have broadened my understanding of myself and my potential. More than anything, I appreciate God and the way He has taken the principles that were planted in the soil of my heart when I was young, stretched and built upon those truths, and caused them to grow and produce fruit as I have walked through the countless array of life experiences that the Lord has chosen to set before me.

I want you to be successful. I don't need to know the specific passions that pulse through your soul or details of the vision that consumes you. As long as your passions are pure, wholesome, and helpful to yourself and to others, I want to see you prosper. In fact, God has called me to devote myself to that very purpose. I want to see you achieve everything God has fixed in your heart, overcome everything that hinders you from pursuing it, become the person that God created and destined you to be, and finish the unique course in life that God has set before you.

I hope the material that follows will help you do just that. I believe that it will because one of the fundamental truths that I have learned from my mentors and encounters with life is that your thinking—invisible and intangible—is destined to produce your life's actualities—physical and tangible. Your thoughts are destined to become your realities. Let me explain this amazing concept in the pages that follow.

CHAPTER 1

THE BIGGEST PROBLEM
IN THE WORLD

The biggest human temptation is to settle for too little.
—Thomas Merton

hat is the biggest problem in the world today? Is it terrorism? Is it poverty? Is it global warming? Is it war? What is it?

If you were to ask a hundred different people to answer this question, you would get a hundred different answers. And, after much discussion, all those people would probably be forced to admit that there is no definitive answer to your question. They would probably be forced to agree that any answer, including their own, is nothing more than an opinion. There is no objectively correct answer to an open-ended question like that, they would say, at least not an answer that could bring any consensus. A person's answer would depend on individual experiences, on the perspective from which he or she views the world. A person's answer would depend on his or her environment as well as priorities, belief systems, and values.

But I disagree with this kind of politically correct response to such an important question. I believe that this question does have merit. It does have an answer, especially for those of us who live in the world's most developed nation. I might let people in some of the world's more impoverished countries get away with a different response because they live in a completely different world than the one that you and I occupy. They deal with a different set of circumstances than we do in more advanced cultures. For those of us who live in a free and prosperous country, the answer is absolute: The biggest problem in our world today is that most people have no purpose for their lives. Like corks bobbing in the open sea, people are lost, and they are floating aimlessly through life—victims of every breeze and current. They see no reason for their lives because they have no vision for them. Because they have no vision, they have no direction.

Why do I say that this is the biggest problem? Because this is the root cause of every other problem in those cultures where a person determines his or her own course in life! A person with a vision for the future has no time for drugs or alcohol. A person with focused motivation has no interest in crime. A person with purpose beating in his or her soul isn't easily distracted by self-destructive behaviors, doesn't respond to the surrounding circumstances in violent ways, and is inclined to work hard and do the right things in order to successfully navigate both the challenges and the opportunities the vision creates. In other words, a person with a vision for life becomes part of the solution for mankind—not part of the problem. That person solves the dilemmas that life places in his or her path instead of creating more problems for the rest of us and is more than willing to deny him or herself today in order to enjoy the benefits of those sacrifices tomorrow.

How many times have you heard that old, familiar story—especially while watching the Olympic Games or the Super Bowl Pregame Show—about an athlete who started out poorly in life, then had a "pivot point" experience that set that athlete on a straight path toward personal greatness? How many times have you heard the same storyline about some of the world's greatest musicians, inventors, artists, and entrepreneurs? They started life badly and made some really poor choices that resulted in a lot of personal internal suffering and a lot of hardship for others. But then, the athlete or musician or artist had a moment when the lights came on and a vision was birthed and a life purpose was discovered. From that moment on, basketball became that young man's launching pad to greatness, or music became that young lady's vehicle to wealth and fame. Then the praise and acclaim quickly followed, and someone who was part of society's problem became part of society's solution for the problems that it collectively confronts.

A PERSON WITH A VISION FOR LIFE BECOMES PART OF THE SOLUTION FOR MANKIND—NOT PART OF THE PROBLEM

Until that "epiphany," that person was going to wander aimlessly through life and into things that would destroy the individual and create hardship for others. However, people with clear vision for their lives focus on that vision to the exclusion of all lesser distractions and are undeterred in their passionate pursuits of the dreams that consume their hearts.

What's more, they aren't ordinarily controlled by the motivations that drive lesser people to do the things that they do. They aren't envious, for instance, so they aren't consumed with taking things that belong to other people (robbery and theft). They aren't angry, so they aren't intent on harming other people or inflicting pain and suffering upon them (violent crime). And they are disciplined, so they have neither the time nor the inclination to yield control of their lives to outside agents (drugs, alcohol, and gangs). They take responsibility, extract all the talents and abilities that are latent within them because these gifts are their "tickets" to significance and success. They safeguard the special abilities that God has entrusted to them and squeeze out every drop of potential that they can possibly surrender.

Confucius once said, "The will to win, the desire to succeed, the urge to reach your full potential . . . these are the keys that unlock the door to personal excellence." Confucius was right. To rise above the mediocrity that permeates our world today, a person must possess a desire, a motivation, and a driving ambition to do something exceptional with his or her life. A person must possess a motivation to achieve significance. But what we rarely consider in this fast-paced world is the thing that gives rise to these kinds of noble virtues. A young man doesn't just accidentally develop a deep desire to do something meaningful with his life while he is sleeping in his bed one night. A young woman doesn't just inadvertently sprout the attributes of self-discipline and patience while she is riding the bus home from school one day. The qualities that cause them to emerge from the masses and to create specific blueprints for their lives are the byproducts and outgrowth of strong personal visions that beat deep within their souls.

For the most part, people who do bad things to themselves and others are people who are dissatisfied with their lives or bitter toward a world that they believe has deprived them of their due rewards. But people with vision and purpose for their lives are people who have no time for such nonsense or for the distractions that can divert them from their goals: substance abuse, obsessive behavior, obesity, illiteracy, bad habits, or anything else that can damage them personally, harm their relationships, or restrain them in their ascent to greatness. So I believe the best way to solve all the problems that currently plague our world is to solve the root problem first, solve the underlying problem so all the offshoot problems will eventually solve themselves, and help each and every person identify the God-given purpose for his or her life. After all, a self-disciplined person is a person society will not have to discipline. A self-motivated person will contribute positively to society— make "deposits" not "withdrawals" from the storehouse of humanity.

FOR THE MOST PART, PEOPLE WHO DO BAD THINGS TO THEMSELVES AND OTHERS ARE PEOPLE WHO ARE DISSATISFIED WITH THEIR LIVES OR BITTER TOWARD A WORLD THAT THEY BELIEVE HAS DEPRIVED THEM OF THEIR DUE REWARDS.

In reality, however, very few people in America or any other advanced economy have vision. Very few see any real possibility for life that is better than what they have right now. Very few see themselves as capable of doing great things or making names for themselves. People don't believe that they matter, that they count. And this is why so many of them drop out of school, join gangs, turn to drugs, resort to violence, migrate toward crime, abandon their families, and live off the government instead of thriving through the use of their own potential. They look around and they don't see many of their friends succeeding or making a difference, so they conclude that they won't be able to do anything meaningful either. Statistics back them up.

In fact, here's an interesting statistic that may help you appreciate the fact that the biggest problem in our world today is the problem of self-perception and personal motivation, not the lack of opportunity. Are you aware that, in the United States, only 4 percent of the population will ever achieve success? That's right! In the wealthiest nation on earth, only 4 percent will ever be able to completely support themselves financially. According to the United States Department of Health and Human Services, only about four out of every one hundred Americans will ever achieve financial independence, perhaps the best all-around indicator of personal success.

I first became interested in statistics related to success during the presidential campaign of 2012. If you will recall, percentages were being tossed around every day by Republican nominee Mitt Romney and President Barack Obama, who was running for reelection. While Obama talked about the 1 percent who were paying too little in taxes and the 99 percent who were paying too much, Romney talked about the 47 percent who were too dependent on the government. For the first time I can remember, we were looking at the American population primarily in terms of percentages. That motivated me to do some research of my own. What did I find?

I found that, in the United States, if you take one hundred young adults who are born with similar talents and intelligence and under similar circumstances, all of these young adults will tell you that they want to be successful. And even though their definitions of "success" may differ slightly, there will be one common element—the desire for financial security and independence.

All one hundred of these people will possess a strong desire to reach that place in their lives where they can pursue their passions and prosper while doing it. In addition, all will actually have the confidence that they can achieve what their hearts desire. They will believe that they can rise to the top and attain the ultimate for themselves and their families. They will be filled with optimism and hope and walk in the assurance that they have what it takes to achieve their hearts' goals.

But as time progresses, some will rise to the top, and others will fall to the bottom. Some will soar while others will sink. By the time they all reach retirement age, only one of them will actually be rich (the "1 percent" that President Obama mentioned). Three more will be financially secure, but as many as fifty-one will struggle all their lives just to get by—eighteen of them working beyond retirement age just to keep a roof over their heads and food on the table. And twenty will end up depending on government support—food stamps, Medicaid, or housing assistance—just to survive.

So the obvious question becomes: What went wrong? Why did so many of these people—fairly equal in talent and zeal when they started out in life—fail to achieve their goals? Why did so many of them fail when all had the resources they needed to succeed? Why is there such a disparity between the outcomes these people wanted for their lives when they were young and the outcomes they actually achieved? Why will an astounding two-thirds of the American population retire with less than $25,000 in the bank? Why will only 4 percent of Americans succeed while an astonishing 96 percent fail to reach the most basic financial goals they set for themselves? That is a question that demands an answer.

I love to see that look of excitement that is so commonplace on the face of a child who is consumed with tomorrow's hopes or a young adult who is taking initial steps toward building a family or career. But I hate to see that predictable look of cynicism that is ubiquitous on the face of a grown-up who has been hardened by the repetitive setbacks he or she never anticipated—that look of calloused indifference. Instead of thriving, these people are merely surviving. Instead of advancing, they are nursing the wounds of a lifetime of retreat from the battles they have lost along the way. And they have plenty of war wounds—relationally, financially, spiritually, and emotionally— to show for their failed efforts.

When people fail to reach even the first rung on the ladder of success, that sets in motion a series of events that can lead them to despair, resulting in behaviors and practices that will surely rob them of their potential and guarantee years of regret. It can lead them to despondency, resulting in practices that inevitably place a burden on society. Their hopes and dreams are dashed because they fail to meet any of their goals. They give up on themselves and become pessimistic toward life and cynical toward the world. Their declining enthusiasm predictably leads to further failures, and these accumulated defeats ultimately drive them to a place of dejection, where nothing really matters except their own physical survival and the feeding of their shortsighted appetites. Consequently, they become a drain on the world around them rather than a benefit. Worse, some even lose their lives.

Obviously, as I have stated, success means different things to different people, but in the United States, a person always starts life with a dream. You can ask any child, "What do you want to be when you grow up?" and you will receive a solid, unwavering response. It doesn't matter whether the child's a boy or a girl, rich or poor, white or minority, highly intelligent or average in mental capacity. Every child will possess a vision for his or her life. But as time progresses these children realize that their dreams are eluding them. They lose heart and begin to "settle" for the circumstances life has handed them. Abandoning the active pursuit of those possibilities they envisioned for themselves, they undergo a downward transition in their thinking for a reason which I will explain in the pages that follow.

They fail to lend their full potential to making the world a better place through their unique contributions, and they definitely fall short of enjoying the full benefits of the lives God created them to enjoy.

So again, the greatest problem we have in our country today and in much of the industrialized world is that millions of people have no direction for their lives, no definable goals and no reason to do anything productive with their time, talents, and resources. Not only are they suffering psychologically and financially, but the rest of us are suffering as well because we often must bear the added weight of caring for them.

In fact, I believe there is abundant evidence to prove this, but it's buried within the financial statistics that we see and read every day. They show the symptoms of a malady that plagues our country but not the cause of these symptoms. It takes a little research and logic to connect all the dots and to see the clear pattern. We have to look beneath the surface to find the cause for the weeds that are sprouting on the surface of the soil.

For instance, according to *Business Insider* (June 22, 2011), only half of Americans have managed to save at least one month's income during the course of their lives. Unfortunately, like many analysts of social economic behavior, *Business Insider* doesn't tell us *why* these people haven't saved any money. Because of my own past experiences and intimate acquaintance with the weaknesses of humanity, I know why. Most people consume all their disposable income on things they want today. They see everything as a necessity and feed all their short-sighted appetites right now while those appetites are crying out to be fed with no grand vision for the future that would motivate them to deny their current cravings in order to finance their future dreams.

And according to the Heritage Foundation, the typical American family living below the poverty line owns two color televisions, a DVD player, and a PlayStation. Each owns a game system like Xbox or PlayStation, a refrigerator, oven, stove, microwave, washer and dryer, and an electric coffeemaker. Almost half have a built-in stereo system, nearly 40 percent own a personal computer, and a whopping 80 percent own a cell phone, which, as you know, isn't cheap by anyone's standards. So while the household incomes of all these families are low enough to qualify them for government assistance, they still have enough available cash to live at a standard that would place them far above the vast majority of people living in undeveloped countries. They can find the money they need to buy the things that they want but not the money to start a business or pursue an education, even though the government would be willing to help them with these two things, as well.

People who are living beneath their potential opt for electronic devices over a college education, not because they are stupid or incapable of doing better. It's because they have no burning passion within their hearts that would motivate them to postpone these simple pleasures in favor of achieving their goals. People today—especially people living in America—will spend their money on everything imaginable, but they won't spend their money to create better lives for themselves—to learn or improve themselves. They have no vision. They cannot "see" anything worth the sacrifices that they must make in order to achieve their dreams. That is why so many people fall short of the goals they had for themselves when they were children.

Here's another interesting financial statistic that will drive home this point: Did you know that 317,000 waiters and waitresses in America have college degrees? What does that tell you? That tells me that the job market is pretty lousy right now. It also tells me that most of these young people had no vision for their lives when they entered college. They failed to plan ahead and studied things that did not prepare them for legitimate careers. When it comes to travel and when it comes to life, a journey with no direction will eventually take you to Gilligan's Island where an astounding 73 percent of college graduates work in professions unrelated to their college majors.

A surprising 57 percent of American households don't even have a budget. People live on budgets when they want to reduce their current spending so they can finance their future dreams. But most Americans don't have any future goals other than retiring rich. And unfortunately, that isn't a legitimate goal, as we have seen because only one in one hundred will actually achieve it. To most Americans, retiring rich is a pipe dream they expect to realize later in life, yet it isn't connected to reality or to any realistic plan for making it happen.

There's a story that was posted online by Charles H. Chandler of the Ministering to Ministers Foundation, and I believe it makes my point rather poignantly. It seems that there was a young boy named Tommy who lived in a small Midwestern town shortly after World War II. Tommy was the only child of two parents who loved him very much but had limited financial means.

Tommy was infatuated with circuses. So when he learned that a circus would be coming to town, Tommy set his heart on going. Tommy's parents, seeing the obvious determination in their son's eyes, decided that they would make whatever sacrifices were necessary to send their son to the circus.

IIIIIIIIIIIIIIIIIIIIIIIIIIIIIIIIIIIIIIIIIIIIIIIIIIIIIIIIIIIIIIIIIIIII

WHEN IT COMES TO TRAVEL AND WHEN IT COMES TO LIFE, A JOURNEY WITH NO DIRECTION WILL EVENTUALLY TAKE YOU TO GILLIGAN'S ISLAND WHERE AN ASTOUNDING SEVENTY-THREE PERCENT OF COLLEGE GRADUATES WORK IN PROFESSIONS UNRELATED TO THEIR COLLEGE MAJORS.

Finally, the day came for Tommy to fulfill his lifelong dream. On the day when the performers were set to arrive and the circus was scheduled to begin, Tommy finished all his chores early, showered, put on his best clothes, and rode his bicycle three miles to town to watch the parade. When Tommy got to town, people were already lining the streets. And in the distance, Tommy could hear the sounds of the band that he knew would be leading all the animals and performers down Main Street to the place where the tents were already erected.

Tommy was gripped with an excitement that could not be contained and eventually was rewarded because elephants followed the brightly colored band, and lions and tigers roared from their cages as they passed by. Tommy's eyes were as big as saucers as he watched the trapeze artists and other performers give limited exhibitions of their skills. Tommy was in a literal state of ecstasy as his dream came true before his very eyes.

Finally, the clowns brought up the rear in much the same way that Santa Claus would conclude a Christmas parade. The clowns were Tommy's favorite part of the circus, and for the first time in his young life, he was watching a sea of real clowns pass before him, displaying their skills while wearing their brightly colored attire.

As the last clown passed by, Tommy did something rather strange. He abandoned his cherished spot on the sidewalk, walked straight up to one of the clowns, and handed the clown the money his parents had given him for admission to the circus. Then Tommy jumped on his bicycle and peddled all the way home. He went to town to see the circus, but he settled for the clowns instead.

Too often, Tommy's story becomes our story. His experience becomes ours. Tommy started out with a grand vision for what he thought would be the greatest day of his young life, but he quickly settled for something less. People are still settling for less than they really want from life. They have bought into the lie that the clowns are as good as it gets; the path of least resistance is the path they were destined to travel.

We all start our lives with the God-given hope that they will be great. We enter first grade with a childlike expectation that all our dreams will come truc and all we imagined for ourselves will actually happen. But as the years pass, we learn to "settle" for less and less. We lower our expectations and become content with less than our hearts have told us we can actually squeeze out of life.

But here's the good news: This problem can be solved. This dilemma has a solution. In fact, the solution is inexpensive; it won't cost anyone anything, and it won't require any taxpayer funding or charitable support. In addition, it's simple; it is easy to understand. However, it must be grasped and applied—on an individual basis—in order to be effective.

Join me as I explain this "formula" for success that can enable any person to live the ultimate life as long as that person is willing to understand the formula and apply it to his or her situation. What is this amazing formula, and how does it work? Read on.

CHAPTER 2

COURAGE, COWARDICE, AND CONFORMITY

I can't give you a sure-fire formula for success, but I can give you a formula for failure: try to please everybody all the time.
—Herbert Bayard Swope

n the opening chapter, I had a lot to say about success and failure. But here's the question we need to ask: What is success, and what is failure? Obviously, failure is the opposite of success, but what is success? What are the exact circumstances that make for success?

Once again, if you were to ask a hundred different people to explain success or to describe the circumstances that lead to it, you would get a hundred different answers. The best definition flows from a compilation of statements made by a number of highly accomplished people. Success is the steady, gradual, and incremental achievement of a meaningful goal, the relentless climb toward the vision that resonates within a person's heart. Success is not the ultimate achievement of a personal vision because a real vision for one's life can never be fully achieved. It is constantly evolving and diverging into new areas as unforeseen opportunities arise and new information is gleaned. Success is realized when a person's most heartfelt dreams gradually unfold as that person does the work and makes the sacrifices to manifest them.

The person who is making progress toward the vision is a successful person; the person who is not making progress toward something that is personally meaningful and significant is a failure. Therefore, all of us are successful in some areas of our lives and unsuccessful in other areas. When it comes to a person's overall life, success must be measured from within, by the standards that person has set. Success must also be measured from without, by the objective standard of whether that person is making measurable strides and observable steps forward in the pursuit of those goals.

On the march to significance, a person with a dream will encounter many obstacles along the way, some of them human in form and some of them circumstantial. The biggest obstacles are the ones people create for themselves through their own limited thinking. Therefore, people who want to be among the top achievers must be willing to think differently than the people around them because, as we have seen, the vast majority of people in the world are thinking in unsuccessful ways. Unfortunately, that kind of stand-alone thinking is rare because it requires courage.

Nothing is more important in the journey to success than courage. The most common—yet invisible—impediment to courage is conformity. If you really think about it, "conformity" is the opposite of "courage" just as "failure" is the opposite of "success." A soldier who stands and fights when all the other soldiers are running for cover is the soldier who wins the Congressional Medal of Honor. That soldier refused to conform to the other soldiers' actions.

Likewise, the student who dares to speak up and confront her professor for the views he is expressing in his political science class is definitely courageous, but she is courageous specifically because she is doing what the other students in her class are unwilling or afraid to do. She is standing alone, rejecting the comfortable path. She is thinking differently than the people around her and acting differently than the people who follow the lead of their friends.

If you were around in 1986, you might remember that in April a sudden power surge during a reactor systems test destroyed Unit 4 of Chernobyl's nuclear power plant in northern Ukraine, just south of the border with Belarus. As a result of the destruction, massive amounts of deadly radioactive material were released into the atmosphere. To this day, nobody knows for sure how many people died as a result. The estimates range from a few hundred to several thousand.

||||||||||||||||||||||||||||||||||||||||||||||||||||||||||||||||

IF YOU REALLY THINK ABOUT IT, "CONFORMITY" IS THE OPPOSITE OF "COURAGE" JUST AS "FAILURE" IS THE OPPOSITE OF "SUCCESS."

In the midst of that tragedy, certain exceptional people rose to the challenge, among them three volunteers who jumped in to keep the disaster from escalating. Three Russian workers—Alexi Ananenko, Valeri Bezpoalov, and Boris Baronov—volunteered to suit up in scuba gear and enter a large pool of highly radioactive water that was accumulating in a flooded chamber. Their goal was to open a stuck gate valve, release the trapped water and thus avoid an inevitable explosion that would have released even more radioactive material into the environment.

In the article "The Real Story of the Chernobyl Divers" posted at History.com, author Andrew Leatherbarrow attests that the search for the necessary valve was like one for a "needle in a haystack," but they were able to locate it before the molten reactor core above them had melted its way down through the ceiling. If not for the bravery of these three courageous men, a thermal explosion would have led to a lot more death and destruction.

Yet as it is with all displays of courage, this act of heroism revealed two undeniable attributes that were present in these men: bravery and nonconformity. These men became heroes because they were brave, but they were brave because they were willing to think and act in a way that set them apart from the rest of the people around them. They obviously viewed life and death—and their roles in each—differently than the other workers at the Chernobyl power plant. To become successful, therefore, you must demonstrate stand-alone courage in all your thoughts and actions. Reject the conventional wisdom of friends, relatives, teachers, and icons who try to influence you on a daily basis, standing instead on your own beliefs when these people are thinking in less than noble ways or marching together down a path that leads to nowhere. When the actions of people—even the majority of them or the most admirable—are not good, you must be willing to take the risks associated with walking your own path. After all, when you are wearing red in a room full of people clothed in earth tones, every eye will be upon you and the criticism will abound.

In the previous chapter, I proposed that the biggest problem in the world today is the fact that most people lack purpose, vision, and direction for their lives. Beneath this pervasive social problem of aimless living is an underlying thought pattern of conformity that gives rise to this mindset and causes it to spread from person to person like some sort of moral flu.

Something about human nature makes us want to follow the herd, even when the herd is wandering around in circles or marching in unison over a cliff into the abyss below. In thought and action, we mimic others more than we want to admit. We subconsciously know that it is safer to simply get in line and submit to the mass conformity that compels most other people to do what they do with their lives. Deep inside, we want to break ranks and do something extraordinary with our finite time on this planet. Unfortunately, we lack the courage to take this bold step because we might fail, and the rest of the flock might laugh at us or reject us or even banish us from the sheepfold.

When you think like everybody else, you will end up like everybody else, and this is why a child's vision for his life grows dimmer with the passage of time and eventually dissipates into mediocrity and conformity, falling short of achieving the dream. We like to believe that we are unique individuals, exceptional. When we are born, we are! But because of the "failure" mentality that we allow to permeate our minds as we make our way through life, we end up putting our uniqueness on the shelf and conforming to the thought patterns and behaviors of those around us without even realizing what we are doing and without thinking about the ultimate outcome of the lives of the people we mimic.

Just look at the statistics that I mentioned in the opening chapter, and you will see that I am right. At the present time, there are more than forty-one million people in this country who are over the age of sixty-six years and two months, and most are financially dependent on others for their basic necessities. I find it amazing that human beings can learn to walk without being told they need to walk and talk without being prodded to do so. But a person cannot learn to think for himself with enough creativity to avoid the financial fate that awaits the vast majority of the people who live in this country. When it comes to the most important aspects of life, a person will often follow the crowd down a dead-end road of compliance rather than walk his own course toward his own definition of success. He will not think things through for himself, and that is sad.

Acting like the 96 percent—the people who fail to meet all their goals in life—won't help you meet your goals in life. If you want to succeed, you will have to think and do things differently than these people think. This principle applies to every facet of life—from parenting to investing and from eating to strengthening your marriage. If you want to be successful, you are going to have to do the opposite of what the masses of people are doing. Perhaps that is why Warren Buffett, the most successful investor in America today, makes nonconformity the centerpiece of his investment strategy. "A simple rule dictates my buying," Buffett once explained. "Be fearful when others are greedy, and be greedy when others are fearful." In other words, if you want to succeed, do the opposite of what the unsuccessful people are doing.

Although children are perhaps the best ambassadors for personal vision and hope, they are the worst ambassadors for individuality and nonconformity because children, more than adults, would almost rather die than stick out from the crowd. They want to dress and talk like their friends and listen to the same music that their friends listen to. Socializing is more important to a child than oxygen, and it's nurtured through conformity. It is very difficult, therefore, for a child to be unique, and that is why a child's dreams are eventually abandoned.

An "inversion" takes place, though, as a person progresses from childhood through adolescence to adulthood. As the need for social acceptance increases, the need for personal exceptionalism decreases. And here's the irony: While vision is important to children and socialization is important to teens, legacy is the greatest need for adults, especially as they grow older. An adult wants to know that his or her life has counted for something; it has made a difference in the world. Older adults come full circle back to the need for purpose that captivated them as children. But it's what those aging adults did during their decision-making and working years that will determine whether they can fulfill the visions of their childhood dreams and achieve the significance they long for. Unfortunately, during those critical years, the majority of people seem to be more interested in the approval of others than they are in making the right choices for their lives.

You see, the older we get the less we seem to care what other people think about us. Elderly people, in particular, are notorious for their lack of concern for social approval. But during those productive years, when we are earning most of our money and pouring most of our time into the things that arouse our passions, it's the focus of those passions and the wise use of that money that count. Few people at that time in their lives think far enough ahead to find the motivation they need to deny their thirst for approval so they can take paths their friends might not approve of. They conform. Then, as they age, they regret the choices they made, especially the choices regarding money.

Do you want to live an extraordinary life, do extraordinary things, achieve your goals and leave your mark on the world? Then you are going to have to do what other people aren't doing—as early as possible—because any successful investor will tell you that once an investment becomes popular or acceptable, it is too late to take advantage of it. In order to make money, a financier must jump on an investment before the rest of the world catches wind of it. And the same principle applies to the other areas of your life. If you wait for the rest of the world to find value in the things you want to do, those things won't be worth doing any longer.

Conventional wisdom is one of my biggest pet peeves. Those who simply repeat the maxims of copycat thinkers and mimic the actions of unaccomplished people are destined to languish in mediocrity themselves. They will rarely achieve great things because, given time, conventional wisdom will almost always prove false. In fact, if the masses are thinking it, it probably isn't true. And if it is true, it won't be true for long. Society is fickle, and the winds and waves of popular opinion are driven by feelings, not by fact. They are driven by simplistic assumptions, not by genuine knowledge. Today's superhero will be tomorrow's forgotten man. Today's hot trend will be tomorrow's nostalgic memory. Remember leisure suits and legwarmers?

||||||||||||||||||||||||||||||||||||||||||||||||||||||||||||

DO YOU WANT TO LIVE AN EXTRAORDINARY LIFE, DO EXTRAORDINARY THINGS, ACHIEVE YOUR GOALS AND LEAVE YOUR MARK ON THE WORLD?

The popular website Quora offers several examples of conventional "wisdom" that have been proven false in recent years. Among them is the long-standing assumption that salt is bad for your health. It was propagated by professionals and embraced by institutions as prestigious as the American Heart Association. Over time, however, scientists have learned that salt isn't necessarily bad for everyone. In fact, a diet too low in salt is more dangerous for a person's health than a slight excess of salt.

Other products of conventional wisdom that have been disproved over the past fifty years include the traditional belief that a person can catch a cold if she gets chilled and wet. There is no connection between being cold and catching a cold, which is the product of germs, not temperature. Saturn was long thought to be the only planet with rings, but now we know that this assumption is false. And for years, margarine was regarded as a healthier choice than butter, but the opposite has actually proven to be true. Conventional wisdom doesn't always turn out to be so wise, and common sense isn't so sensible, especially when the assumptions that are being embraced are based on ill-founded beliefs rather than attested principles of reality.

Over the years, I have come to doubt most of the common logic of society, especially that opposed to God's eternal laws or that based on the hottest topics in the media that just recently entered the conversation. In fact, I have become so opposed to "group think," I sometimes believe that if I heard an explosion outside my house and opened the door to see everyone running to the east, I would run to the west. I have come to realize that conventional wisdom is usually wrong. The thinking of the masses almost always steers me in the wrong direction, and it definitely takes me to places I do not want to go. It takes me toward failure.

There is nothing wrong with gaining wisdom from those who have some real wisdom to share or following in the footsteps of those who have actually walked a path to success in the past. Most of us, though, conform to the wrong people. We follow the 96 percent who have opinions they have never actually tested in the real world. We follow the herd. We act like the people who are on the front side of success, talking about all the things they plan to do in the future, rather than the people who have actually achieved the dreams that once resonated in their hearts.

People subconsciously opt for conformity over individuality because we are programmed as human beings to seek social acceptance. We are mentally and emotionally wired to seek the approval of those around us. Consequently, the acceptance of the flock can often be more important to us than our own physical survival, our own self-esteem. Feelings of loneliness or isolation can drive people to despair and lead to all sorts of mental problems, so people will literally sell their souls to gain the collective approval that they need without even realizing it.

I am not trying to suggest here that you need to be weird or antisocial, renounce your citizenship in the human race, or withdraw to the mountains of Tibet. What I am suggesting is that you need to make your own decisions in life and learn to think for yourself, especially when it comes to those matters that pertain to your unique, one-of-a-kind purpose. Take action to keep other people from robbing you of your dreams or neutralizing them in your life by redirecting you down senseless rabbit trails. If your friends support you in your pursuit of your God-given dreams, then reconfirm your deep friendships with them and let them be part of your pursuits. But if they require you, overtly or covertly, to change your goals or to modify your values in life, then start looking for more exceptional people to populate your inner circle.

Relationships are important: I am not going to deny that fact. Our relationships are a gift to us from God—vital to a healthy and fulfilling life—but every relationship has a price tag. It costs you something. That is the nature of a relationship. While an unhealthy relationship will deplete you, a healthy relationship will give you, over time, a return on your investment that is at least equal to the price you pay to sustain that relationship. Eventually, if you are not receiving a return on the investment you make in a particular relationship, that relationship is unhealthy for you and should probably be reevaluated.

A healthy relationship will add something to your life. It will improve you as a human being, not diminish you. Make sure you are not sacrificing yourself merely for approval or accolades (better known as "groveling") or throwing away your own dreams just for the crumbs that other people can offer you through half-hearted acceptance of your companionship. Many people will require you to abandon your noblest ambitions in order to win their favor because your noble ambitions will often offend them, confuse them or make them feel inferior. But a person who truly loves you, who is a good person to have in your life, is the person who will support you in your God-given pursuits and nurture the qualities that can help you achieve them. Refuse to surrender your dreams and goals to people who don't value you or your potential. Refuse to offer them as a fool's ransom for momentary popularity. Refuse to "cast your pearls before swine" (see Matthew 7:6).

There is a growing tendency for people to think of themselves as victims. That isn't new, but thinking of oneself as a victim is now more common and socially acceptable than it has been in the past. To make matters worse, this way of thinking is being propagated by the media and proliferated by politicians who know they can capitalize on it to secure a few votes. If you want to cancel your membership in the 96 percent, you also need to avoid the people who encourage you to see yourself as a victim.

The government doesn't control your life, and it hasn't caused your present problems. Wall Street doesn't control your life, and it isn't keeping you from being successful. The police don't control your life, and they aren't hindering you from achieving your goals. Your boss doesn't write the script of your life, and your boss isn't standing in your way. The uncomfortable truth is that you control your own destiny. You are the product of all the habits you have formed, the choices you have made. You are the byproduct of all the people you have invited into your life to counsel you and to steer you with their advice. If those four lonesome souls out of every one hundred people in America can secure their own success in spite of the limitations that confront them, you can do the same. Your destiny lies in your own hands.

While some may view this harsh reality as bad news, you should learn to view it as a solid foundation for your future. If you can make a mess out of your life by making unwise decisions that flow from a lack of personal direction and bad associations, then you can turn that ship around by starting to make better choices and decisions that flow from a more precise vision for your future. If people feel like they are victims, it's only because they don't have any direction. A cork floating on the open seas obviously feels like it is being controlled by the winds and the waves, but a vessel on the same waters that has clearly defined ports of origin and call is a vehicle that will never feel controlled by the waters, the weather, or any of the creatures of the sea. Neither will the individual who has a clear purpose for his or her life.

Everywhere you turn you will be reminded that you are a victim—of this particular group of people or that particular institution, your parents' poor parenting skills, or your controlling employer. You're a victim of a poor educational system, big business, big banks, big oil, and Big Brother. You're a victim of the anger or complacency or timidity that are part of your ethnic heritage. According to the pundits, none of us are in control of or are responsible for the outcome of our lives. We are all "victims" at the mercy of forces that are stronger than we are and people who are smarter than we are.

If you can't manage to find a person, group or institution to blame for your miserable plight in life, you can always blame your circumstances. Or heck, you can just blame your ancestors or a sad situation that occurred in the past to your great-great-great-great grandparents. We would rather accept any rationale—even the alignment of the planets and stars—to explain our personal failures than the rationale that makes the most sense: My life is the product of my own choices. My choices are the product of my own thinking. Like the 4 percent, I, too, can succeed in life. The problem, therefore, must not lie with any of the scapegoats I've been blaming for as long as I can remember. The problem must lie with me. I'm thinking like the wrong bunch of people, and I've somehow aligned myself with the wrong crowd.

Let me ask you a few simple questions: Why do you work? Why did you choose your current profession and job? Why did you go to college? Why did you choose the person you decided to marry? Why did you get married and have a family? Most people would have a difficult time answering these simple questions. They don't really know why they made these choices other than everyone else was doing them. But the only people who truly succeed in life are those who intentionally plot their courses and then work every day to walk those courses to their predetermined conclusions, who set goals for themselves that are rooted in their own unique purpose and then pay the price to achieve them.

A successful person says, "I'm gonna do this," and then starts the process and actually walks the walk instead of just talking the talk. He's the man who is building the business that he always dreamed of building or the woman who becomes the chairperson of a major corporation because she knows she can guide that company into the 21st century. It is the man who is maintaining the farm that his father and his grandfather built because that is what he truly wants to do with his life. It is the woman who is an amazing wife and mother because that is what she envisioned as her highest purpose and calling.

A successful person is anyone who is pursuing a predetermined, worthwhile goal and doing a good job because that is the goal he or she deliberately set his sights on when starting out in life. Only about four in every one hundred people will ever set a goal for their lives and then work deliberately toward it. Others will fail because they're more interested in popularity than success, in being accepted than being right. They want to be *part* of the flock instead of *ahead* of the flock, though they would never admit it. They want to play it safe and not take the risks associated with sticking out from the crowd.

Natalie Coughlin was a competitive swimmer who participated in her first Summer Olympic Games in 2004. At her very first Olympics, she won five medals (two gold, two silver, and one bronze) and broke one world record. Coughlin would return to the Olympics four years later to become the first American female athlete to win six medals in a single Olympics. Shortly after the 2008 Olympic Games in China, Coughlin was forced to endure two shoulder surgeries to repair damage that occurred as a result of the overuse of her muscles.

The conventional wisdom that dominated sports at that time said that Coughlin's career was over. At the very least, it would be diminished. But Coughlin refused to walk away from her passion for swimming. Instead, she took an eighteen-month break to heal and to rehabilitate her muscles. She didn't want to take the traditional route when it came to the rehabilitation of her broken body. Instead, she decided to train with University of California coach Teri McKeever, who introduced Coughlin to a whole new approach toward getting her body back in shape. Rather than focusing on rebuilding her shoulders and arms, Coughlin focused on her legs. By learning to do Pilates, this eleven-time Olympic medalist was able to strengthen the connection between her arms and her legs through the core of her body, thus enhancing her physical abilities for competitive swimming.

Of course, the peddlers of conventional wisdom warned against this unproven method, but after eighteen months, Coughlin was back in the pool, winning three more gold medals at her first international competition following her surgeries. And at the 2012 Olympics Games, Coughlin won her twelfth Olympic medal, tying the record for the most Olympic medals for a female US athlete.

If you want to be great, you have to stop being average. If you want to be uncommon, you have to stop being common. If you want to go places where few people have gone, you have to stop following the herd to the places they frequent. If you want to be different, you have to think differently. Stop thinking like the 96 percent. It's like Dave Ramsey, the noted author and financial advisor so often says, "If you will live like no one else, later you can live like no one else."

Deny yourself certain things today; live like other people would never be willing to live. Reject the status quo and get intentionally out of step with the drumbeat that guides most people through life. Muster the courage to place your own internal passions above your need to be like the people around you, and you'll eventually find yourself doing the things that others only dream about doing and going places where others can only dream about going as they make their way home from work each day, stopping at the mailbox to grab another fistful of bills so they can go inside and figure out a way to keep things afloat for another thirty days.

I stated in the first chapter that financial independence is perhaps the best indicator of success, but it's not the only indicator. I have used finances as the barometer because the vast majority of people include financial security as one of their personal goals. They want to do what they love to do, and they want to get rich doing it. Financial prosperity by itself is not the perfect measurement of a successful life because some people place little value on material things. They want to be safe and secure, able to support themselves and their families, but they don't really care about amassing great wealth.

‖‖‖

MUSTER THE COURAGE TO PLACE YOUR OWN INTERNAL PASSIONS ABOVE YOUR NEED TO BE LIKE THE PEOPLE AROUND YOU, AND YOU'LL EVENTUALLY FIND YOURSELF DOING THE THINGS THAT OTHERS ONLY DREAM ABOUT DOING AND GOING PLACES WHERE OTHERS CAN ONLY DREAM ABOUT GOING

A truly accurate definition of success, therefore, must be larger and broader than just a financial definition. That is why I define success as the steady, incremental achievement of any goal that is noble and meaningful. To me, successful people walk a steady path toward a predetermined dream because they deem that dream to be a worthy destination, one that will bring satisfaction and significance, as well as the ability to provide for themselves and their families. Regardless of the money attached to a goal, the one chasing that goal must be considered a success if the end goal is honorable and that person is making measurable progress toward its achievement.

Only about one in twenty-five people will ever experience that kind of satisfaction—deliberately focus on an honorable pursuit and then do the work and pay the price that is necessary for completing that pursuit—and the feelings that go with crossing the finish line in a race that is run with purpose. Only about 4 percent of Americans will experience the ultimate life. That is a sad statistic that needs to be improved.

Fortunately, it *can* be improved if people will start paying attention to the root cause behind this sad reality and start thinking about themselves and life in a whole new way. The secret to changing course in and changing the outcome of your life is to change the way that you think about your life. If you don't have a destination in mind when you raise your anchor and set out for the open seas, you will end up traveling in circles until you eventually run out of fuel and float ashore on some uncharted island around which all the other aimless vessels of the sea have found their graves. A destination for your life is the starting point for success. So let's take a look at how you can identify your God-given reason for being and define your unique destiny in the world.

CHAPTER 3

THE POWER OF GOALS

*If you don't know where you are going, you
will probably end up somewhere else.*
—Laurence J. Peter

Years ago, when I first became aware of the concept of "vision" and its critical role in the pursuit of success, I quickly realized that I had discovered something that was truly amazing. Obviously, I was not the first person to discover this key to the ultimate life, nor would I be the last. But as I began to grasp this concept for myself, I was awakened to the absolute power of vision in a person's life. A person's vision (or lack thereof) can tell you just about anything you would ever want to know about that person and go a long way in helping predict the future outcome of that person's life, as well. It can tell us whether the person is going to be a giver or a taker, a leader or a follower, a high achiever or a deadbeat, a success or a failure.

Just think about it! Think about a successful person you know and try to figure out how he or she became so successful. Was it hard work that took that person from obscurity to success? Well, in a sense, yes. Work is a positive virtue, and it is definitely one of the building blocks of a successful life. But if you try, you can probably think of a lot of people you know who work hard and never seem to get ahead; they always seem to be treading water. Hard work, therefore, is not the key; it is the byproduct of something else.

What about intelligence? Did it take that person from the bottom to the top? Yes, in a way. Without intelligence, a person cannot achieve very much in life, and without understanding, a person cannot apply knowledge. You can probably think of a lot of people who were really smart when they were in school, yet they failed to achieve what their peers thought they would when they voted them "Most Likely to Succeed." So intelligence is not the key to success either.

Although wisdom and understanding, hard work and sacrifice, discipline and focus all play important roles in a person's journey to the top, none of these virtues could be classified as the "key" to success, the "secret ingredient" that separates the common from the uncommon and the good from the great. Something else undergirds a person's noble qualities and causes that person's positive attributes to function together in a way that can make success attainable (and even predictable). That underlying thing is a "vision" that is reflected in a person's lifelong goals. Nothing, therefore, is more needful and powerful than the goals that propel one toward a reason for being and the vision that gives birth to those goals.

Have you ever taken a long trip? How did you get to your destination? You undoubtedly took a car, bus, train, plane or maybe even a boat. Whatever form of transportation you took, you boarded that vehicle with a clear understanding of where it was going. You read the sign at the gate, and you listened carefully to the public address announcer to make sure you were boarding the vehicle that was headed where you wanted to go because every vehicle that is leaving one place is heading toward a defined destination somewhere else. Each trip is completely planned and mapped out in advance; all the fuel and resources needed for the journey are on board. Every crewmember, whether one or a thousand of them, knows exactly where the vehicle is going. There is neither uncertainty nor argument. The vessel's destination has been determined before the landing gear leaves the runway or the anchor is even raised.

||||||||||||||||||||||||||||||||||||||||||||||||||||||||||||||||||

SOMETHING ELSE UNDERGIRDS A PERSON'S NOBLE QUALITIES AND CAUSES THAT PERSON'S POSITIVE ATTRIBUTES TO FUNCTION TOGETHER IN A WAY THAT CAN MAKE SUCCESS ATTAINABLE (AND EVEN PREDICTABLE).

Imagine what life would be like if there were no signs and no public address systems to help us find the right bus or the right flight, if your destination weren't printed on your ticket and determined in advance. Imagine what life would be like if the drivers of buses and the pilots of spaceships had no predetermined courses in mind and could just drift to their hearts' content to wherever the elements happened to take them. The world couldn't function, could it? Nothing would work properly. Every endeavor would fail.

That's exactly the way it is with most people. They have no aiming point, destination for their lives, vision or goals to help them achieve a meaningful purpose in this world. Instead, they just start the engines and let the airplane fly until it runs out of fuel somewhere over the ocean and crashes into the water below. And then they wonder what went wrong. They stare in amazement at all those other airplanes that seem to be traveling somewhere rather than flying in circles, and they grow envious as they try to figure out why those planes are actually achieving something that they can't seem to achieve.

I have a friend (let's call him James) who once told me about a couple of astonishing things that happened to him while he was in high school. It seems that James attended school during the 1960s in a small town in the Deep South, where people related to one another quite differently than they do today. James's story is fascinating in spite of the passage of time and quite relevant to our topic. In fact, James told me this story in the context of a discussion we had regarding the subject matter of this chapter, and it is a great illustration of the point I am trying to make.

It seems that James's father (let's call him Nelson) had a lifelong friend named Bobby. They had been close friends since they were kids. Shortly after Nelson got married, Bobby got married, too. Nelson had his first child, and Bobby had his first child. Nelson had his second child, and Bobby followed suit. When their children were still quite young, Bobby and Nelson would spend time together, and the children would play in the next room or take naps together in the crib. But eventually Bobby joined the Air Force and moved far away.

Occasionally, Bobby and his daughters would come back to his small hometown to visit his parents. But he no longer visited Nelson because Bobby's transient lifestyle had caused them to lose contact. Eventually, Bobby worked his way up through the ranks, becoming an officer and a pilot. One tragic day, however, Bobby's family was notified that he had been shot down over Vietnam. Later, Bobby was declared dead by the Air Force. Nevertheless, Bobby's children—even as teenagers—continued to visit their grandparents.

During his junior year of high school, James was introduced to a girl who lived in a town ninety miles away. While chatting with her, James learned that she came to town regularly to see her grandfather and grandmother. That's when James asked this young lady if he could take her out whenever she was in town, and she said, "Yes." So every time this girl came to town to visit her grandparents, she would call James, and James would pick her up and take her to a movie or a high school football game or to some other place where teenagers tend to congregate.

During one of these visits, James happened to mention the young lady to his father, Nelson, who had asked his son a few questions about this new girl in his life. When James mentioned the girl's name, Nelson quickly realized that this was Bobby's younger daughter, the little girl who used to sleep in the crib while James and Bobby's older daughter played together in the house. James remembered nothing of this, and Nelson never mentioned Bobby or his daughters to James after Bobby moved away. In addition, the girl didn't know anything about Bobby's lifelong friendship with Nelson. So the coincidence presented by these unfolding events was truly amazing, and it was almost like James and Bobby's daughter were destined to meet one another.

The possibility of James meeting the daughter of his own father's childhood friend, a girl who lived almost one hundred miles away and who used to play in his house when she was a small child, is extremely remote. But, even though I found this story fascinating, the best part about the story for me was the analogy I could draw from it and the life application I find there.

It seems that while James was in his senior year of high school, Bobby's younger daughter contacted him and invited him to the beach the following week since she was going with her mother and her sister. By that time, the girl's mother, Bobby's widow, was dating another Air Force officer who also was planning to drive to the beach that week to spend some time with her. So the mother and her two daughters planned to rent a vacation house near the beach, and the Air Force colonel would stay at a nearby motel.

James and a friend took advantage of the invitation and decided they too would find accommodations close by.

On the night James and his friend arrived at the beach, all six people gathered at the vacation house for dinner. Before the two younger boys took the girls out to a movie while the mother and the colonel went for a walk on the beach, the colonel offered to let James and his friend share his motel room since it had two double beds, and he had a sleeping bag in his car. The colonel told James the name of the motel and the room number (this was back in the days when they still used metal keys to unlock motel doors) and said he would leave the door unlocked. Because James and his friend could not find any other motels with vacancies, after the movie, they headed for the Chesterfield Inn and the colonel's room. Unfortunately, they could not remember the room number. While one of the boys thought it was Room 311, the other one thought he remembered the colonel telling him that he was staying in Room 414.

The two boys crept up and down the hallway on each floor of the motel, gently turning the doorknobs on each door to see if one of the doors would open.

Finally, around two o'clock in the morning, they found an unlocked door. Upon quietly opening the door, all they could see in front of them was darkness, and all they could hear coming from the room was the sound of gentle snoring. Was this the right room? Was the snoring coming from the colonel or from someone they didn't know? The only way they could tell for sure was to quietly close the door behind them, wait for their eyes to adjust to the darkness, then get on their hands and knees and crawl over to the bed next to the window so they could see who was sleeping in that bed. My friend, of course, was extremely relieved to find the colonel sleeping there.

What does this humorous little story have to do with *Mindset Matters*? Well, I share it with you here because this is exactly how most people travel through life. They jiggle the handle on this door; then they jiggle the handle on that door, hoping something meaningful will open up to them. They crawl through the darkness and test the waters to see if they have made the right choices and happen to be traveling in the right direction. Every momentous decision in their lives is a shot in the dark. There is no consistency to their choices, no strategy behind their actions, no clear room number (destination) in mind. In fact, they can't even remember the address of the destination they are looking for. They're just feeling their way through the darkness, hoping that they somehow magically stumble across the pot of gold that could suddenly make their lives better. And they hope to avoid getting arrested in the process.

People who get things done are driven by something invisible. Deep within their souls there is something intangible, yet undeniable, that compels them to dig a little deeper, work a little harder, go a little farther, and give a little more. They are happy, yet never content, fulfilled, yet never satisfied, balanced, yet sold out to the one thing that seems to provide them with a reason to get up every morning and do what other people seem unable or unwilling to do. They are determined, audacious, focused, and undeterred. They are self-denying, self-controlled, self-motivated, and self-disciplined because there is something that keeps them pointed in the same direction every day,

||||||||||||||||||||||||||||||||||||||||||||||||||||||||||||||||||

PEOPLE WHO GET THINGS DONE ARE DRIVEN BY SOMETHING INVISIBLE.

no matter what happens around them or to them. They are consumed by a passion and driven by a dream that never seems to go away, leave them alone, fade, or fluctuate. These are the men and women who make the world work, who give birth to new ideas, who solve the world's problems. They give us the innovative products and services that make our lives better. These titans inspire us because there is something inside them that just won't let them be average. It burns like an eternal flame and pushes them toward a level of excellence in all areas of their lives that most people can only admire from afar. Vision is the common motivator of all those who do great things.

Compare these amazing people with the masses who never seem to get out of first gear, and it becomes obvious that the difference is not culture, race, gender, intelligence, wealth or the opportunities that these people's parents gave them in life. The difference is drive. Those who live beneath their potential have had most of the same opportunities that the world's greatest achievers have had, but the high achievers had something else that could not be measured, weighed, or quantified. It was indefinable. They had passion that flowed from a dream, a hunger fueled by a personal desire to do something extraordinary, a catalyst within their souls that ignited the talents God gave them. And this inner compulsion enabled them to focus on one thing to the exclusion of all unworthy distractions.

With our nation's ever-expanding victim mentality and ever-growing entitlement culture, it is possible to live a reasonably comfortable life without ever making an effort to do anything with one's time or talents. The harder we work as a society to keep the weak from failing, the more difficult we make it for the strong to succeed. The more we do to make life effortless for those who won't engage, the more we encourage people to live their lives without purpose. Who wants to live that kind of life? That's not living, and it is certainly not "ultimate" living. Such a mentality destroys not only the individual human soul but society as well.

When the Soviet Union was the greatest existential threat to the United States and communism and capitalism stood in stark contrast to one another, someone wisely observed that communism is simply the practice of the government stepping in to deprive a person of his or her God-given right to fail. Predictably, therefore, communism itself failed because no person, society, human institution, or government can guarantee success to the person who lacks vision. No power in heaven or on earth can guarantee success by insulating a person from failure or by depriving a successful person of his due rewards in order to reassign those rewards to someone who did not earn them and does not appreciate what was required to obtain them. Success is a personal endeavor—not a collective one—an individual pursuit, not a "right" guaranteed by society. Genuine success can only be achieved when a solitary human being is consumed by something that is personally meaningful and motivates that person to walk a predetermined path to achieve it.

Fortunately, in this country, we offer a certain level of security to our citizens. We don't let people die in the streets from starvation, even if those people make a deliberate choice to live on the streets. There is a definite baseline to the amount of suffering we will tolerate but no predetermined ceiling that sets limits on how far a person can rise. It is up to each individual to determine how far above the baseline he or she wants to ascend. Some will rise quite far and quite rapidly, others will rise more slowly, and still others will fail to rise at all or will actually travel in a downward direction. In the United States, the path taken, the distance traveled, the height obtained, and the outcome of one's pursuits are defined by a person's commitment to goals that stem from internal vision for that person's life.

This is why goals are so important; they change the outcome of a person's life. People with goals accomplish more and go farther than people who have no goals. Vision is the overall driving motivation of a person's life. It is the "shining city on a hill" that is a person's destination, but goals are all the tiny steps that a person must take to climb the mountain that stands between him and that city. Goals are the battles that a person must wage in order to clear the path toward the destination that enthralls her heart—the landmarks along the journey. A climb up a mountain consists of thousands of tiny steps, and a climb toward a vision consists of a thousand tiny goals. People reach their destinies by reaching their goals, and achieving goals is a clear indication that they are making progress toward their destinies.

Goal setting and vision, therefore, are the keys to success in life because people become what they think. That's right, we become what we think and what we think about—not what others tell us we can be. Even the ancient writings of the Bible teach us that there is a direct connection between personal success and the way we think, and many secular writers have also commented throughout the centuries on the undeniable relationship between thinking and outcome, demonstrating to us the unchanging nature of this universal principle.

For instance, a little more than three thousand years ago, King Solomon, recording his astute observations of life, wrote, "For as (a man) thinketh in his heart, so is he" (Proverbs 23:7, KJV). The way a man thinks determines what he becomes. The way a man (or woman) thinks determines that person's choices, and those choices determine actions which eventually determine the storyline of a person's life. The person who thinks he can, can and who thinks he can't, can't. She who thinks she will, will and who thinks she won't, won't. As we think, so are we. As we think, so we become.

To make it clear that this principle is more than just the musings of an ancient king and to prove that the connection between thinking and outcome is global in its scope and timeless in its application, let me invite you to consider the observations of some people not mentioned in the Bible who have impacted our world in both past and present times.

Look at Helen Keller who said, "The most pathetic person in the world is someone who has sight but no vision." This is quite an interesting statement from a woman who was both blind and deaf! Tony Dungy, the first African American coach to win the Super Bowl, said, "The first step toward creating an improved future is developing the ability to envision it." And Marcus Aurelius, Roman Emperor from 161-180, said, "Our life is what our thoughts make it."

Each day, you will write one more chapter in the story of your own life. As the chapters pile up, a plot will begin to emerge and eventually end with the chronicles of the life you have lived. Regardless of the elements you have faced or the obstacles you have encountered thus far, you have been the author of your own story, the architect of your own fate. You are the person who made all those choices that eventually took you where you ended up, who said all those things that produced the good and the bad in your life. You are the one who has written every word of every chapter of the history of your own life, but you only could have written what you knew, and you only could have known what you imagined. So you, my friend, for better or for worse, have been the "imagineer" of your own destiny. You are the "imagineer" of the storyline that remains to be written.

Consequently, if you want to become rich, you have the power to become rich, but you have to start thinking like a rich person. If you want to be successful, you have the power to become successful, whether you seek to be a businessman, a salesman, a scientist, a musician, a husband, a wife, or an "A" student. But you won't become any of these things—succeed at anything you attempt to do—if you don't have goals that can lead you to the places you want to go. You won't have any real goals to guide you if you don't think about the things you want to be and do with your life. You will eventually become what you think, what you imagine in your own heart and mind.

About a thousand years after King Solomon made his notable observation regarding the power of personal vision, Jesus of Nazareth made another authoritative statement about the force that gives rise to a vision. Speaking about faith, Jesus said, "All things are possible to him who believes" (Mark 9:23, NASB). So if you believe that something can happen for you and you think about it often and in positive ways, you are much more likely to achieve it than the person who thinks about nothing or things that don't matter. However, if you don't believe that a certain thing can happen for you and you think about that thing rarely or in negative ways, you probably will never realize that goal in your lifetime. It's as simple as that.

The "secret" to the ultimate life isn't really a secret at all; it's just something we rarely consider. Our thoughts direct our lives and determine everything about us. It's not about your circumstances. It's not about the people around you. It's not about your age, gender, financial status, or the color of your skin. It's about the presence or absence of a vision in your life and the thoughts that either give rise to a budding vision or destroy that vision before it can grow and yield its fruit. It's about *minding your own head.*

|||||||||||||||||||||||||||||||||||||||||||||||||||||||||||

THE "SECRET" TO THE ULTIMATE LIFE ISN'T REALLY A SECRET AT ALL; IT'S JUST SOMETHING WE RARELY CONSIDER.

In his play, *Mrs. Warren's Profession*, Irish dramatist George Bernard Shaw said, "People are always blaming their circumstances for what they are. I don't believe in circumstances. The people who get on in this world are the people who get up and look for the circumstances they want, and, if they can't find them, make them." So it's pretty obvious to me that great people have discovered the primary ingredient of success. They have discovered that the outcome of one's life is linked, not to outside forces, but to one's own internal thinking. Just as a person's hair and skin color are linked to an internal genetic code and a person's success or failure is linked to an internal belief system, so a person's destination is linked to his or her focus. We eventually become what we think, and we eventually achieve what we think about in our hearts and in our minds.

It stands to reason, therefore, that the person who thinks about a concrete and meaningful goal will be more likely to actually achieve that goal. That is what he ponders in his mind, so that is what he will become. But the opposite is true, as well: The person who has no goal for her life, no idea where she is going or what she was created to pursue is also destined to become what she thinks about: nothing. Instead of possibilities, she will only see problems. Instead of open doors, she will see barricades and obstructions. Instead of excitement, her life will be marked with anxiety. Instead of hope, worry!

Warren Buffett, one of the most successful businessmen in history, is a renowned investor and the CEO of the fourth-largest company in the United States. But did you realize that, by his own admission, Buffett spends about 80 percent of his working hours reading and thinking.

Some people in hot pursuit of success believe that activity is the most important prerequisite for success. Don't get me wrong; action is a good thing. You can never achieve your goals unless you are willing to put action behind your beliefs and undergird your thinking with the force of hard work. But in my opinion, people with enormous potential are more likely to fall short of their goals by failing to think than by failing to act. Many are so action-oriented, they are impulsive, and impulsive actions are sometimes more destructive than no action at all.

So Buffett spends a lot of time just thinking, and he is not alone. According to Brian Scudamore, founder and CEO of his own multimillion dollar company, there are other highly successful people out there who do the same thing. "AOL CEO Tim Armstrong, for instance, makes his executives spend 10 percent of their day, or four hours per week, just thinking," Scudamore says. "Jeff Weiner, CEO of LinkedIn, schedules two hours of uninterrupted thinking time per day. Jack Dorsey is a serial wanderer. Bill Gates is famous for taking a week off twice a year just to reflect deeply without interruption."

So this is more than merely my opinion—my idea—as a success coach. Thinking must always precede action, not the other way around. As Abraham Lincoln once said, "Give me six hours to chop down a tree, and I will spend the first four sharpening the axe." Our actions flow from our thoughts, but our actions also follow the path of our thoughts. If our thoughts are poorly developed, our actions will reflect our limited thinking. If our thoughts are lofty and focused, our actions will lead to meaningful results. Thinking is the necessary prerequisite to accomplishment, and our accomplishments always take the shape of the thoughts that produced them.

The person who thinks about nothing will become nothing, and the person who thinks about "little" things will become "little." But the person who thinks great thoughts and pursues great ideals is one who is destined to become great. It might take those people some time to figure out how to navigate the potholes in the road to success and deal with the nemeses who stand between them and their dreams, but in the end, they will get where they are going because people become what they think. People achieve what they think about.

||||||||||||||||||||||||||||||||||||||||||||||||||||||||||||||||

THE PERSON WHO THINKS ABOUT NOTHING WILL BECOME NOTHING, AND THE PERSON WHO THINKS ABOUT "LITTLE" THINGS WILL BECOME "LITTLE."

Why is this true? What makes this principle work? How does a person become what he thinks, and why does he become what he thinks about? As we continue to explore this phenomenon, let me give you an analogy that you can easily understand so you can fully grasp this amazing reality of life. Once you capture this concept in your heart and make it part of your life, you will never be the same again.

CHAPTER 4

HOW THOUGHTS BECOME REALITY

You can't live a positive life with a negative mind.
—Joyce Meyer

S o how does this principle work in the real world? How do a person's thoughts shape his or her life? Why does a man eventually become what he thinks, and how does a woman ultimately achieve what she thinks about?

Let me explain this phenomenon by borrowing a brilliant analogy from Earl Nightingale, one of America's earliest motivational speakers and writers. I found Nightingale's analogy, based on the biblical concept of "sowing and reaping," in one of his lectures from 1950. In his comparison, Nightingale points to a real-life situation that all of us can understand, a situation that perfectly parallels the activity of the human mind. He compares the mind to farmland and the cultivation of the mind to agriculture.

Suppose that a farmer has some rich, fertile land, Nightingale explains. Once the land is plowed and made ready for planting, the farmer has a choice to make. Depending on the time of year and the environmental limitations of the land he intends to cultivate, the farmer gets to choose what kind of seeds he will plant in the fertile soil.

The land doesn't care—it has no opinion—what type of seeds the farmer plants. The land is simply the receptacle for the seeds designed to give the farmer a return on his investment, whatever that investment might be. Whatever the farmer plants, he will get it back—in abundance. The human mind is a lot like this farmer's land: It comes into this world basically empty, waiting for somebody to fill it with something. It is fertile and capable of producing an abundant harvest. In fact, science hasn't even begun to grasp the inexhaustible resources of the human mind, but the mind starts out like the land, empty and waiting to be sown with seeds of information, waiting to produce an abundance of the same kind of "seeds" that are planted in it. Both will embrace the "seeds" that are sown into them and reproduce those "seeds" in exponential numbers.

Either owner can plant seeds of negativity or optimism. The land doesn't care, and the mind doesn't care. However, the outcome of a person's life, like the harvest the farmer will produce each year, will be based completely on the choices that person makes regarding the kinds of seeds to sow.

A seed looks like a tiny, insignificant speck of matter. In reality, it is one of the most amazing things in the world. Inside that seemingly insignificant seed, there is an invisible "code" that God placed there to give that seed all the information it will ever need to reproduce itself. Invisible information will tell that seed whether it should grow into an oak tree, a corn stalk, or a cotton plant, and the seed never gets confused. It has its marching orders that clearly define what it is supposed to do, produce, and be in life. Once that tiny seed is placed in the soil, it begins to do the one and only thing that God designed it to do, execute the specific "assignment" that it was created to complete.

Our minds are like that fertile soil, capable of producing a bountiful harvest. They won't produce anything until some seeds—designed to impart either life or death—are planted, germinate, grow and eventually produce the harvest that they were designed to produce. The thoughts we allow to take root in our minds are the "seeds," just like the farmer's corn or beans are the "seeds." Like the seeds, the thoughts we plant in our minds are preprogrammed to produce a certain outcome for our lives—either abundant living or frustration and lack of personal fulfillment.

|||||||||||||||||||||||||||||||||||||||||||||||||||||||||||||||||||

OUR MINDS ARE LIKE THAT FERTILE SOIL, CAPABLE OF PRODUCING A BOUNTIFUL HARVEST.

Let's suppose that the farmer decides to plant half his land with corn seed and half with castor bean seeds, which are extremely poisonous. This is an imperfect illustration because corn and castor beans grow in different environments and flourish in different types of soil. Nevertheless, for the sake of the point I want to make, let's use this comparison anyway.

Let's imagine that the farmer plants his seeds side by side, waters them, and takes care of them the way that he should. Eventually, half the farmer's land will produce corn and the other half will produce castor beans. The land doesn't know what it is producing; it doesn't care. It was created by God simply to give back to the farmer the same thing the farmer plants in the soil, so the farmer gets an abundant crop of corn and another of castor beans.

This is the biblical concept of sowing and reaping. The apostle Paul explained, "Be not deceived; God is not mocked: for whatsoever a man soweth, that shall he also reap" (Galatians 6:7, KJV). Our lives, therefore, are the products of the seeds that we sow into them, the deeds that we perform, the words that we speak, and the thoughts we allow to permeate our minds on a daily basis. The harvest you reap when all your work is finished will be the harvest you produced for yourself when you chose the seeds you wanted to plant in the rich, fertile soil of your own mind. Farmland can produce an abundant harvest of corn just as easily as it produces an abundant harvest of castor beans, a harvest of food just as readily as a harvest of poison. And the mind can produce success just as easily as it produces failure. The choice is up to the one who plants the thoughts. Agriculture is absolutely fascinating to me. How a tiny seed can be buried in the ground until the elements cause it to fall apart and then emerge from the soil to become a mighty oak or a pine tree, a redwood or a maple, is beyond my comprehension. The human mind is even more amazing than a seed and much more mysterious. It is capable of retaining information and doing things scientists simply cannot explain. And yet, we are told that we humans use only about 10 percent of our brains.

Imagine, therefore, the potential of the human mind if it could be totally unleashed. As you think about the nearly limitless potential of your own mind, realize that it is neutral. It comes into this world empty, waiting to be fed, waiting to be sown with seeds of information. Eventually, the mind will regurgitate exponentially the seeds that are sown into it. The life of a person will become precisely the outgrowth of what has been sown—by others as well as each individual sower. Because a person grows and matures and becomes capable of differentiating between positive and negative thinking, each person must ultimately be responsible for everything his or her mind absorbs, retains, and reproduces.

Each and every day we make decisions regarding the thoughts we will plant, fertilize, and nurture in our minds and the thoughts we will reject. Whether we plant success or failure, goals or confusion, purpose or conformity, righteousness or evil, our minds, like the farmer's soil, are created to give us a return on our investments. A harvest is coming, and all of us are destined to reap what we have sown into our own minds.

So decide right now what kind of person you want to be, where you want to go, and what you want to do with your time in this world because the most important decision you will ever make is the decision regarding what you want your life to look like when it is fully matured. What is it you want to achieve? Do you want to build your own business, find a cure for cancer, publish your own book, or be a mother who raises three healthy and amazing children?

It doesn't matter what you decide, what specific seeds you choose to plant in the fertile soil of your mind. The only thing that matters is that you plant the right kinds of seeds and that you water, tend, fertilize, and work hard to take care of them. If you do, those seeds will eventually sprout and yield an abundant harvest for you that will carry you where you want to go in life. This is a reality—a fixed law of nature. There is no way this cannot work for you. The thoughts you sow into your mind are the thoughts that will eventually give rise to something tangible and lasting because you are destined to become the physical manifestation of the invisible thoughts that dominate your thinking.

Perhaps you are familiar with *Romeo and Juliet*, the famous tragedy and love story by William Shakespeare that has been performed on stage and film more times than anyone could count since it was written more than four hundred years ago. If you are familiar with the basic plot of this play, you probably realize that a series of unplanned events eventually lead to the suicides of the two young newlyweds who are the center of attention in this drama. What you probably haven't considered about this play is that *Romeo and Juliet* is nothing more than a series of really bad decisions made by two young people, crazy in love with one another, and the reversal of just one of those decisions could have saved their lives and dramatically changed the outcome of the story.

In fact, all of Shakespeare's plays have this one element in common: They are nothing more than a long series of events that transpire as a consequence of the leading characters' actions which determine the outcome of the play. Before each character acted, that character managed to reveal his or her thinking through his or her spoken lines. At any point, therefore, a key player in the unfolding plot of any

Shakespearean play could have made a different choice by thinking differently, and that would have produced a different outcome for everyone involved.

Romeo and Juliet takes place in the Italian city of Verona where two noble families are embroiled in a bitter and sometimes violent feud. The Capulets and the Montagues are warned by the prince of Verona that the next person who disturbs the peace is destined to be punished by death.

In the context of this warning, Romeo, a Montague, disguises himself and attends a party at Capulet's home. There, Romeo sees—for the first time—Juliet, the fourteen-year-old daughter of Capulet. But Romeo is soon discovered, and he leaves the party, returning later that evening to meet Juliet privately on the balcony outside her bedroom. There on the balcony, the two exchange vows of love.

Soon afterward, Romeo tells Friar Laurence what has happened to him, and the friar agrees to conduct a wedding ceremony for the two love-struck teenagers. The next day, under the pretense of going to confession, Juliet meets Romeo and the two of them are married in a ceremony conducted by the friar. The two newlyweds decide to keep their marriage a secret, at least for the time being.

While this is occurring, a young suitor by the name of Paris tries to make Juliet his bride. Paris appeals successfully to Capulet for the hand of his daughter, so Capulet puts a lot of pressure on his daughter to marry Paris. As a result, Capulet and Juliet argue passionately about her future as Capulet insists on Juliet agreeing to this marriage.

With the tremendous pressure from her father bearing down upon her, Juliet returns to Friar Laurence to seek his help. He gives her a potion that will cause her to appear dead for some time. He tells her to agree to marry Paris and then to drink the potion so her family will think she has died. Then she can elope with Romeo, and they can start a new life together away from their families' influences. In the meantime, Friar Laurence tells Juliet that he will inform Romeo of the scheme, so Romeo can be ready to take Juliet away.

After returning from her meeting with Friar Laurence, Juliet tells her father that she will submit to his wishes and marry Paris, so Capulet hurries to arrange the ceremony for the very next day. But Juliet drinks the potion, and, thinking her dead, the Capulets take Juliet's body to their family crypt.

Never receiving word of this complicated scheme, Romeo hears that Juliet has died. He obtains his own poison from a local apothecary and goes to the Capulet crypt to die next to his young bride. While there, however, Romeo encounters Paris, and the two of them fight. Romeo kills Paris, drinks the poison, and dies next to Juliet, who soon awakens from her slumber to find Romeo's body next to her in the crypt. When Friar Laurence arrives to tell Juliet what has happened, she refuses to leave with him. Instead, she kills herself with Romeo's dagger, and Friar Laurence is left to tell both families about the tragic series of events that led to this unimaginable outcome.

The outcome of this play, like the outcome of a person's life, was not an accident or a coincidence. What actually led to the tragic deaths of Romeo and Juliet was a long series of poor decisions and unwise actions by everyone involved that flowed from poor judgment and unwise thinking. However, a change in just one of the actions taken by Romeo or Juliet could have radically altered the outcome of their lives. Unfortunately, their thinking drove the decisions that they made, and their thinking was unsound.

What would have happened, for instance, if Romeo had never approached Juliet on the balcony of her residence, if he had thought things through and concluded that the pursuit of this girl would be dangerous and ill advised? If Romeo had really pondered the difficulties that would surround a relationship with Juliet and had made the choice to walk away, he may have longed for her for a while, but he would still be alive to pursue those things he really wanted to do with his life.

Or what if Juliet, after seeking the friar's help, had decided not to deceive her family with a dishonest and elaborate charade, but instead had decided to join with Romeo to invite both their fathers to the friar's residence where they could tell the men about their love and their recent marriage?

What if Friar Laurence had given the newlyweds better counsel, Romeo and Juliet had decided to wait to get married, Juliet had discussed her deceptive scheme with Romeo before moving forward with it, and Romeo had decided to do something—anything—other than kill himself at the Capulet family crypt? What would have happened if Shakespeare had decided to write a comedy instead of a tragedy?

Unfortunately, what happened is what happened, and it is forever sealed in the archives of English literature because, right or wrong, the characters in Shakespeare's play made the decisions that they made at the time, and each of those decisions set in motion a series of events that led to the outcome of the story. Because Shakespeare's characters are a little different from characters in most modern literature (they think out loud through their spoken words), we can learn from this tremendously popular play that a person's thinking leads to certain predictable actions which lead to certain predictable outcomes. Nothing good could have come from all the violence, hatred, lying, and deception that dominated the thinking of the Capulets and the Montagues, so Romeo and Juliet, as well as all the people around them—from Juliet's father to Friar Laurence—reasoned stupidly when it came to the choices they made regarding their futures and the futures of those that they loved.

So as the farmer stands there beside his plowed field, trying to decide what kind of seeds he wants to plant in the soil, he has a decision to make. The dirt beneath his feet doesn't care. The farmer can think wisely when he makes his decision, or foolishly. He can think with the future in mind, or solely for the moment. But his thoughts will determine what kinds of seeds he will plant in the soil which will determine the kinds of produce he will be eating and selling at market.

The farmer, however, also understands the three laws of agriculture that will guide the process along, so he makes his decision based on these three laws. We would be wise to follow his example because the laws of life are the same as the laws of agriculture. The farmer (and the person making decisions for his life) will reap *what* he sows, *after* he sows, and *more* than he sows. It's the way God made things. These are the unchanging laws of God's creation.

||||||||||||||||||||||||||||||||||||||||||||||||||||||||||||||||||||

THE FARMER (AND THE PERSON MAKING DECISIONS FOR HIS LIFE) WILL REAP *WHAT* HE SOWS, *AFTER* HE SOWS, AND *MORE* THAN HE SOWS.

If the farmer plants corn, he will reap corn. If he plants castor beans, he will reap castor beans. The farmer will reap *what* he sows. Likewise, you will reap what you sow into your own mind. If you spend all your time around negative people, absorbing their thinking and adopting their attitudes, if you profess negative things, read negative material, and watch negative or worthless programming all night long on television, you will eventually reap what you sow. You will reap a life of negativity and meaninglessness. You will reap nothing beneficial from your spare time or your latent talents. But if you spend most of your time around uplifting people, absorbing their thinking and adopting their attitudes, if you believe and profess positive things, listen to inspirational music, and entertain yourself with good thoughts and think about good things while you pursue wisdom and knowledge, you will eventually reap a life marked with happiness, fulfillment, and significance. You will reap *what* you sow.

But the farmer will also reap *after* he sows, and this is the hard part of the equation. Wouldn't it be nice if a farmer could buy a piece of land and then wake up the next morning with a field full of soybeans just waiting to be picked? Unfortunately, the laws of agriculture don't work that way, and life doesn't either. Before there can be a harvest, the farmer must plant something in the soil and wait for it to grow. Before that he must purchase the seed and do a whole lot of hard work to get the soil ready for planting season.

The ground must be plowed, the soil must be fertilized, the weeds and insects must be managed, and the seeds must be sown before the farmer can receive anything for his efforts. And what's more, the farmer does all these things upfront without any guarantee that his labor and his expenditures will produce anything for him. The uncontrollable and unpredictable elements of life could send him a heat wave or a late frost, a drought or a flood. Birds could invade his fields at any time, vandals could destroy the tender shoots, or the farmer could be injured or get sick and fail to complete the work that is necessary for producing a bountiful harvest. Before a farmer can reap anything, therefore, he must take some risks by investing his time and his resources in a venture that is worthy of his best efforts, and then deal with all the potential threats that could undermine what he has envisioned. He reaps *after* he sows, and you will reap after you sow, too.

In fact, the things you are reaping today in your life are the direct results of the things you planted in the past. They are the result of the things you planted in your relationships, in your career and in your mind. Likewise, the things our nation is reaping today—both good and bad—are the direct results of the decisions our leaders made in the past and the things that they "planted" for future generations to reap. For better or for worse, here's what this fixed law of God's creation means for you at this point in your life: In the same way the things you are reaping today are the consequences of the choices you made in the past, so the things you reap in the future will be the consequences of the choices you make today, and those flow from the thinking that dominates your mind right now.

Life doesn't happen by accident, and there is no such thing as "luck." There is an irrefutable connection between actions and outcomes, between thinking and actions. Your thinking, therefore, determines your outcomes: in finances, your relationships, your career, and your health—every aspect of your life. The seeds you are sowing into your mind today are germinating and growing, and they will eventually produce a harvest. So this one thing you should know: Whatever seeds you are sowing today, you can bet your bottom dollar that one day soon you are going to be picking the fruits and the vegetables that those seeds are programmed to produce. Good seeds bring about harvests of good things. Bad seeds bring about harvests of bad things. Your past is evidence enough that this fact is true, so wise up and realize that you are destined to become what you think.

The farmer reaps *what* he sows, and the farmer reaps *after* he sows. Here's a third law of agriculture that every person needs to grasp: The farmer will also reap *more* than he sows. The man who plants one tomato seed will pick dozens of tomatoes from the vine. The woman who plants one kernel of corn will pick dozens of ears of corn and thousands of kernels of corn from the stalk that seed produces. The laws of agriculture demand that the seed gives a bountiful return when it is planted in the soil, and the human mind is designed to do the same. If you sow good things into your mind—wisdom, knowledge, and understanding—you will reap, over the course of time, a bountiful and abundant harvest of good things, and if you sow trash into your mind or sow thoughts of idleness or despair, you will reap, over the course of time, destruction in your life. You will never have purpose, direction, or significance. And you certainly won't have success.

My advice to you is to forget about the past. You can't do anything to change yesterday, and the only good things you can derive from your past failures are wisdom and experience. You certainly can change tomorrow. If you sowed castor beans and your farmland is completely covered with poisonous plants, you can plow those plants under and start over. You can starve the castor beans altogether by letting them die from neglect, and you can start again with better seeds. You can plant some corn in the fertile soil of your mind and start reaping a bountiful harvest of something wholesome and nutritious.

The fixed laws of nature, particularly the laws of agriculture, are guaranteed to work. They cannot fail because they are inflexible. Begin to think about the things you want to do, the places you want to go in life, and the goals you want to achieve. Spend your time with people who think about the things you want to accomplish and who talk about the things you want to do. Feed your mind with the information and inspiration you will need to walk that path. And start picturing yourself in your mind's eye as having already achieved the goals you have set before you.

If you want to be an executive in your company, for example, picture yourself sitting in your corner office, looking out the window onto the street below. If you want to be a surgeon, picture yourself in the operating room, helping a sick patient regain his health. If you want to be a professional entertainer and you have the necessary talent to be one, picture yourself standing in front of an overflow crowd as you sing your latest song to the cheers and applause of your many fans. If you want to be a professional golfer, picture yourself sinking a twenty-foot birdie putt on the 72nd hole of The Masters to clinch your first green jacket.

As Nightingale explained more than sixty years ago, every person is the sum of his thoughts. And nothing has changed over the past six decades. People end up where they end up in life because that's really where they want to be. I am where I am today and you are where you are today because that's really where we want to be. I know that's harsh, but it's true. What you thought about years ago is what you are harvesting today. And what you think about today and tomorrow will mold your life and determine your future. You are guided by your own mind.

If you hope to do great things with your life, you need to start appreciating the force of your own mind. Your life is like a nuclear-powered aircraft carrier. It is complicated, expansive, and almost limitless in its power and range. You have within you the mechanisms and motivations to go almost anywhere, do almost anything, and be just about anything you could possibly want to be. But that nuclear-powered submarine is being guided by a single human being. In a tiny little room somewhere inside that mighty ship, there is a solitary sailor at the helm of the craft with his right hand on the wheel. And he is directing the course of that awesome vessel, which has the firepower to destroy a small nation.

||||||||||||||||||||||||||||||||||||||||||||||||||||||||||||||||||||||||||||

IF YOU HOPE TO DO GREAT THINGS WITH YOUR LIFE, YOU NEED TO START APPRECIATING THE FORCE OF YOUR OWN MIND.

That's exactly the way it is with your life. Like the man steering the aircraft carrier, your mind is guiding everything. Your mind is setting your course, determining your speed, and directing the ship of your life, with all its firepower and potential, and it will either run that ship aground or steer it toward its destination. As it is with anything powered by nuclear energy, the results you get will be determined by the way you use that massive power supply. If you use nuclear power in a bad way, it can be one of the most destructive forces in the world. But if you use it properly and channel it appropriately, it can be a magnificent source of energy for your whole life, propelling you toward your optimum potential.

Why don't people know about this, realize that their lives are in their own hands and not the result of circumstances or other outside forces they cannot control? Why don't people understand the power of their own minds, that their lives are the direct result of their own thinking? These are mysteries worth exploring further.

CHAPTER 5

WHY DON'T PEOPLE KNOW ABOUT THIS?

Change your thoughts and you change your world.
—Norman Vincent Peale

W henever the discussion turns to the deeper things of life—things like dreams, goals, and priorities— the conversation gets predictably uncomfortable because it moves dangerously close to the realm of faith. And all of us know we are not supposed to talk about religion or politics.

Even though it may be a little dangerous to discuss your faith with others, the thing that is amazing about the subject of one's thought life is that all religions agree that a person's thoughts shape that person's life and destiny. The various schools of religious doctrine fail to agree on just about everything else in life, but they all espouse the clear connection between a person's thinking and behavior. And all of them connect a person's behavior with the outcome of that person's life.

Those of us who believe in the existence of God believe that we find our origins in Him. This means that we were created for a purpose, a reason. I was not an accident; neither were you. Even though some of us may have been surprises for our parents, we were not surprises to God. We did not catch Him off guard, unprepared or without a plan when we were born. Because our lives have their origins in Him, our lives also have real purpose. This means that you have an assigned destination in life as you travel from your point of origin to the destiny that awaits you. The Architect who fashioned the most microscopic details of His creation did not build a highway through life that takes you nowhere. You came from somewhere, and you are definitely going somewhere. Your life has meaning.

In spite of your origins and God's specific plan, the fact remains that you hold the keys to your own destiny. You are not a puppet on a string, a floating cork in the ocean, driven by the wind and the waves along a random path to wherever you happen to land. You have a will, a brain, a say in the outcome of your own journey. You have been equipped with a moral compass and the power of reasoning that are God's gifts to you so you can plot most of your own course through life to your eternal destiny.

||||||||||||||||||||||||||||||||||||||||||||||||||||||||||||||||||||||||

IN SPITE OF YOUR ORIGINS AND GOD'S SPECIFIC PLAN, THE FACT REMAINS THAT YOU HOLD THE KEYS TO YOUR OWN DESTINY.

Along the pathway, you will be called upon to make millions of decisions, and those decisions will compile to determine the course you plot, the path you travel, the ultimate destination you reach, and the kinds of experiences you will have as you make your way toward the destiny you are forging for yourself because you are God's partner in plotting your direction through life. He has a plan for you, and He will share it if you will allow Him to. In addition, He may even take total control of your life on occasion, so He can sovereignly guide you in the direction He wants you to travel. You, though, will take all the steps, so you will make most of the navigational decisions. After all, you are the person steering the ship most of the time. You are the "helmsman" God has put in charge of your life. So all the tiny choices regarding your voyage will come from you. You can either plot your course according to the master plan your "Captain" has given to you, or you can deviate from that plan and deal with the challenges of the unknown. You will stray from God's path from time to time, even if you don't intend to do so. Then the most important question becomes this: What choices will you make when you encounter detours and roadblocks and other impediments to your forward progress or when you encounter other irresistible opportunities that might cause you to veer off course?

There is significant disagreement among the world's religions regarding the role that God plays in our lives, and there is equal disagreement among the world's Christians regarding the same issue. Does God control most of the details of our lives, or does He allow us to shape our own lives through the choices that we make? Does God predetermine every aspect of life for us, or does He allow each individual to plot his or her own course and determine his or her own path? I believe that God leaves most things up to us as individuals. After all, He told Adam that it was his prerogative to name all the animals (see Genesis 2:19). God didn't care what Adam called them. And the apostle Paul told the widows in the church at Corinth that they were free to marry anyone they chose. God didn't care whom they married as long as they chose husbands who were believers (see 1 Corinthians 7:39). I don't believe that God micromanages our lives.

I believe He gives each individual a unique destiny, which is basically discoverable through inner honesty with one's own passions and interests, and then He leaves most of the day-to-day decisions of life to us, trusting us to follow the guidelines He has given us through His written Word. When we follow those guidelines, we do better; when we ignore them, we fall short of our potential.

Regardless of one's beliefs about the level of God's involvement in one's life, no school of thought can deny that one's decisions affect one's life outcome. In fact, on this one subject every theological discipline agrees: A man becomes what he does, and a man does what he imagines. So our thoughts ultimately shape our lives. If this reality is so universally accepted by all the world's religious thinkers and secular philosophers as well, why don't people understand this important truth? Why don't they even know about it or recognize it as a reality of life?

In American society, where the Christian faith has been predominant, most people are at least acquainted with the Bible. The Bible drives home this concept with clarity and conviction from the opening pages of Genesis to the closing verses of Revelation. Over and over, the Bible affirms the connection between a person's inner thoughts and the outcome of that person's life. The Bible also makes a clear connection between a person's thoughts and eternal destiny.

For example, Jesus said, "It shall be done for you as you have believed" (Matthew 8:13, NASB). In other words, the things that you hold true in your own mind have a way of taking shape in your life. If you believe you can, then you probably can. If you believe you can't, then you probably can't. If you believe you will, you probably will. If you believe you won't, you probably won't. God will do for you what you believe He can do for you. Neither He nor you will do what you cannot believe. From Jesus' statement and the countless other biblical references that support or elaborate on it, we can gather three important truths that we need to remember as we seek to think about those things that can positively shape our lives and take us to places we want to go.

FIRST, THERE ARE CERTAIN FIXED LAWS IN GOD'S CREATION.

God created the laws that govern our universe before He created people to live under those laws. So the story of human history has largely been the story of mankind's discovery of the unchanging laws that God wove into His creation. The human story is the story of how human beings have discovered the laws of nature and how we have learned to utilize those laws to our advantage and apply them in a way that could make our lives better. The natural laws of God's creation have always been there, but until man discovers each of these laws and applies his discoveries to the problems that confront him, he cannot take full advantage of his environment and fully utilize the fixed principles of the universe.

Take gravity, for example. Gravity is a permanent, fixed law of God's creation, and the law of gravity is universal. Gravity works all the time, everywhere, under all circumstances. It works the same in China as it does in Cuba, and it worked the same during the second century BC as it does in this present day and age. You will never hear a news report about a community in the Midwest that had to cancel its annual Veterans Day parade because it had no gravity that day or a battle during any of the world's great wars where soldiers started floating off into space. Gravity is a universal and eternal part of natural law. It has existed from the beginning, and as long as the universe endures, the law of gravity will stand.

But until mankind understood the law of gravity, we could not shape our decisions in a way that could make that law work to our advantage. We did not understand how the moon could hang in the sky or how the sun could rise and set with predictable precision. But after discovering, studying and understanding this fixed principle of nature, we now comprehend the law's implications for our lives, as well as the limitations it places upon us. This knowledge has enabled us, not to control the law, but to appreciate it and utilize it to our advantage. Because we understand the science behind it, we also know what it takes to temporarily and artificially override this law. The laws of nature are more expansive and more fixed than we could have imagined just a few years ago because, as the exploration of space continues, we are finding that the natural laws that work without variance on earth also work without variance throughout the universe. Throughout the universe, for instance, warm liquids will always cool as the temperature drops, and the speed of light will always be 186,000 miles per second. The laws of physics work the same everywhere all the time. This demonstrates, not only order and intelligent design throughout the universe, but also predictability and conformity. We can stand on a firm foundation of truth as we peer into the unknown ages of the future and the expanse of the planets and the stars with full assurance that certain principles will never change. Steady and reliable, certain "rules" are fixed and embedded in the physical universe.

In addition, there is one "language" that is spoken everywhere throughout the universe, clearly applicable throughout the expanse of the cosmos. It is the language of mathematics. Anything that can be measured mathematically here on earth can be measured mathematically at any point in the universe, and the quantification of these things remains the same regardless of where they are measured or computed. To many scientists, this is a strange thing. It makes no sense.

"There is no logical necessity for a universe that obeys rules," says filmmaker Dinesh D'Souza, "let alone one that abides by the rules of mathematics." And yet, the universe does both. It points to one architectural mastermind who both conceived and created everything we know. It points to God. And because God's creation clearly points to His existence and personal involvement in the formation of every physical thing we know and the drafting of every law that governs the universe He has made, we can rely on the conformity of those rules and the eternal nature of those fixed principles as we live our daily lives. There are just certain fixed laws in God's creation that will never waver and never fail.

SECOND, YOU AND I HAVE THE ABILITY TO DETERMINE HOW GOD'S FIXED LAWS WILL IMPACT OUR LIVES.

Colleen Moore has a website where she shares information, advice, and stories about people who have chosen to approach life from a positive perspective. One story that was recently submitted to her website, Mastering Positive Thinking, was a story about a man by the name of Michael.

According to the story, Michael was one of those people who could easily get under your skin. Smiling all the time, happy all the time, he refused to have a bad day or a bad attitude. If something negative happened in his life, Michael would just find a way to extract something positive from it. If somebody said something negative to him, Michael would find a way to change the subject to a more positive conversation.

The woman who submitted the story said that she used to work with Michael and that once she asked him directly, "How can you be so positive all the time?"

Michael explained to her that his attitude was a choice. Simple as that! He said that he had learned from life that good things are going to happen and bad things are going to happen. But he had the power every day of his life to choose whether he would be a positive person that day or a negative person. So he decided he was going to begin every single day of his life by choosing to be positive, regardless of the circumstances that confronted him because they were subject to change, and Michael didn't want to waste his life while he was waiting for those changes.

Years after losing touch with him, the woman began to wonder what had become of him. She conducted a search and soon discovered that

Michael had been severely injured in an accident. It seems that he had fallen sixty feet from a communications tower. That's like falling from the balcony of a six-story building. The woman also learned that, following the accident, Michael had endured eighteen hours of surgery and a lengthy stay in the intensive care unit at the hospital. He had survived the fall, but he was destined to live the rest of his life with discomfort, limited mobility, and several rods in his back.

About six months after the accident, the woman went to visit Michael. When she asked him how he was, Michael responded, "If I were any better, I'd be twins," something he used to say to her all the time when they worked together.

"Do you want to see my scars?" he asked.

"No, thanks," she said, but she did want to learn more about the accident and how Michael survived that terrible ordeal. She also wanted to know what Michael was thinking at the time the accident occurred.

"The first thing that went through my mind was the well-being of my soon-to-be-born daughter," Michael told his former coworker. "Then, as I lay on the ground, I remember that I had two choices: I could choose to live, or I could choose to die." Michael used to tell her that a person's attitude in life was as simple as a daily choice between a positive attitude (life) and a negative one (death).

"Weren't you scared?" the woman asked. "Did you lose consciousness?"

"The paramedics were great," Michael told her. "They kept telling me that I was going to be fine. But when they wheeled me into the emergency room and I saw the expressions on the faces of the doctors and nurses, I got really scared. In their eyes, I read, 'He's a dead man,' and I knew I needed to take action."

"What did you do?" the woman asked him.

"Well, there was a big, burly nurse shouting questions at me," Michael explained. "She asked if I was allergic to anything. 'Yes,' I replied. So the doctors and nurses stopped working as they waited for me to reply. I took a deep breath and yelled, 'Gravity.' Then, over their laughter, I told them, 'I am choosing to live. Operate on me as if I am alive, not dead.'"

So Michael pulled through—seriously wounded as a result of the accident—but fully alive in every sense of the word and fully convinced that his choices made the difference between life and death.

Jesus said in Matthew 8:13 (NASB), "It shall be done for you as you have believed." This tells me, therefore, that there is a fixed law in God's creation. It says beliefs lead to aftereffects and thoughts lead to outcomes. There is a variable to this law, as there are to many of God's laws. While I do not have the power to change the law itself or to choose the circumstances under which the law will affect me, I do have the power to determine how this law will apply to me as an individual. I have the power to control the first half of the equation. I have the power to choose what I will believe and what I will think about. I cannot rewrite this unchanging law or ignore it, but I can make this law subservient to my own needs by selecting the thoughts and beliefs that fuel this law in my life.

The principle here is unyielding. It shall be done for a person as that person has believed. Each individual has the ability to choose *how* the law will work in his or her life because each individual has the ability to choose *what* he or she will believe.

〜〜〜〜〜〜〜〜〜〜〜〜〜〜〜〜〜〜〜〜〜〜〜〜〜〜〜〜〜〜〜〜〜〜〜〜

IT SHALL BE DONE FOR A PERSON AS THAT PERSON HAS BELIEVED.

That means you can build your life on this law. You can "bank" on this law. It's like the laws of agriculture that I explained in the previous chapter. The land is preprogrammed to return to the farmer whatever the farmer sows into the soil, and that is the part of the law that the farmer cannot control. However, the farmer gets to choose what he plants, and that is the part of the law that the farmer *can* control. Likewise, you get to choose the way in which the fixed law of belief will apply to your life because you get to choose what you will think about and what you will believe regarding the things that you think. You can plant corn, and you will reap corn. Or you can plant castor beans, and you will reap castor beans. Likewise, you can think negative thoughts and believe destructive things, and your life will become unproductive. Or you can think positive thoughts and believe constructive things, and your life will become fruitful.

Perhaps you have heard the story about the two nineteenth-century shoe salesmen and their groundbreaking trip to Africa. It seems that, many years ago, a shoe manufacturer in Great Britain wanted to send two of his best salesmen to "scout out the land." It was shortly after the American Civil War, during a time when the British were beginning to make inroads into African culture. David Livingstone, the famed missionary to Africa, was exploring the continent at that time.

The shoe manufacturer simply wanted to know if there might be a need for his shoes there. With the newly emerging relationship between the British Empire and the Dark Continent, this visionary entrepreneur thought a door of opportunity might be opening for him into a new and potentially enormous market.

So the two salesmen were dispatched to Africa. Shortly after arriving there, one of them sent a letter back to his employer in London, saying, "There is no potential here—nobody wears shoes." But the other salesman sent his own letter back to London, saying, "There is massive potential here—nobody wears shoes."

For both of these men, the fixed law worked. But each of these men got to choose what he would believe regarding the things that he saw and experienced. One of the men saw a mismatch between his product and the culture that surrounded him in Africa, but the other man saw an opportunity to market and sell something that was desperately needed by the people he had just met.

You can see, therefore, that many of the laws that govern our lives come with a variable attached to them. The laws work in certain and predictable ways but hinge on choices. The laws of God's universe usually have a "Button A" and a "Button B." Depending on the button you decide to press, you always get what that particular button dispenses. By choosing the button, you choose the outcome and effect that the law will have on your life.

But inherent in Jesus' statement we find a third fact we need to grasp about the power of thought and belief: People simply do not know about this principle. And if they do, they rarely think about it or utilize it to their benefit.

PEOPLE SIMPLY DO NOT KNOW ABOUT THIS PRINCIPLE.

Jesus had to explain to His followers how their beliefs could shape their lives because they had never entertained a concept like this before. Like the rest of us, they did not understand how their own thinking could determine the quality of their lives. This explains why 96 percent of people fail to achieve success; they fall short of their God-given potential. They do not know about this basic reality: The way their lives turn out is determined, not by their circumstances or by other people, economic trends or the government, but by their own thinking and belief systems. A person's paradigm determines the storyline of that person's life.

How would you feel if you suddenly learned that you had just inherited $1 million? You would feel great, wouldn't you? I would be ecstatic. Let me add one small caveat to my question: How would you feel if you suddenly learned that you had inherited $1 million a decade ago? That's right! Ten years ago, you inherited $1 million from a distant cousin who had no children of his own. The executor of your cousin's estate set up an account for you at your local bank and then wired the money to your new account, but the letter he sent to you to inform you of your newfound inheritance was somehow lost in the mail, and you are just now learning about the account.

Would you be happy? If this happened to me, I would be happy the whole day after learning that I had $1 million waiting for me at my local bank. But then, after driving to the bank personally to make sure the money was really there, I would probably start getting a little angry—not at my cousin or at myself or at the bank, but at the situation. I would think back over the previous ten years and ponder how different my life would have been if I had only known that I had that kind of money in the bank.

If I had known that $1 million was sitting in a bank account with my name on it, I could have avoided some of the financial sacrifices I'd made. I could have done a lot of things that I decided not to do at the time. I could have done things for my wife and my son that I did not do, experienced things that I passed up, or purchased a different house. I know I would have developed my career in a different way. I could have blessed a lot of people who needed more help than I was able to provide for them at that time.

I did things the way that I did them because I didn't know what I had. In my make-believe scenario, I didn't have $1 million. If a person doesn't know what he has, he can't use it. Unfortunately, most people are in that same boat. They just don't know what they have. They don't know that they have the potential to fill their heads with the right things and then reap a harvest of success from the seeds they have sown. They don't understand that their thinking shapes their lives and their beliefs shape their destinies—that there is a direct correlation between the things they think about and the things they do, the things they dream about and the things they accomplish. Even though the potential for greatness is right there in their minds, they don't know that it is there. They don't know that they have an amazing "stash of cash" available to them that they can utilize to propel their lives forward.

I know I'm not the first person to tell you that insanity is doing the same thing over and over, hoping that the outcome will be different if you will just do the same old thing one more time. But that's exactly the kind of insanity that fuels this particular phenomenon. When our parents were young, they believed that life would just "happen" for them. They believed they could not possibly fail. But as our parents grew older, they came to realize that they should have thought about life differently, done some things differently when they were younger. So our parents try to teach us how to avoid the pains that they brought upon themselves, to impart to us their wisdom. When our parents try to share their hard won insights with us, we tend to ignore their counsel because we are convinced like they were that life will just "happen" for us. We are convinced that success in life is somehow guaranteed. We are convinced that we are invincible; we cannot fail.

What our parents learned that many of us still don't understand is that failure is the default position in life for those who do not know what they are doing. Because failure is the outcome of most people's lives, success is rare. The person who would succeed in life is the person who understands what he must do differently from the vast majority of the people around him, the 96 percent who will fall short of their goals. He must figure out what constitutes success and what must be done to achieve it. Success doesn't just "happen" to a person, and it won't just fall out of a tree and hit you on the head simply because you were born or because the people in your immediate family are all successful. It is the people who understand the importance of the seeds they plant in their own minds who will end up achieving their goals. The people who comprehend the connection between their thinking and their behavior, their beliefs and the outcome of their lives will taste the ultimate life.

Unfortunately, most people will never know about this principle, so most people won't be able to apply this truth unless someone tells them about it. Jesus told His followers about it, and most successful people will tell their children about it, thus explaining why the majority of the world's successful people come from families that are already successful. But most of the people out there will never understand this eternal law or even hear about it. Like the people who lived under the law of gravity before they knew what gravity was, they won't be able to understand why things work the way that they do in their lives and why they cannot succeed like the people they admire from afar. They won't be able to harness the power of a law that was designed for their benefit because they won't even realize that the law exists or how it is affecting the outcome of their lives.

Shortly after creating the first man and woman, God said something significant and applicable to the subject I am addressing here. Speaking to Adam and Eve, God said, "Be fruitful and increase in number; fill the earth and *subdue* it" (Genesis 1:28, NIV, emphasis mine). This verse intrigues me because it reminds me of all the resources that are imprisoned in the earth, just waiting for our discovery and our efforts to harness them. It reminds me of all the spiritual and natural laws that are out there, just waiting for our investigation so they can benefit our daily lives. It reminds me of all the sources of blessing God has hidden for us in the dirt, in tiny molecules, and in the unexplored regions of the sea and outer space, blessings and resources and knowledge and assets that are capable of dramatically enriching our lives. But it's up to us to discover these resources and utilize them, to understand these laws and apply them for our benefit, to discover the vast wealth that God has placed at our disposal so we can subdue—control—that wealth and put it to work to improve our lives.

Ignorance isn't bliss. If I don't know that a tremendous resource like oil is in the ground beneath my feet, I will never make use of that precious commodity or enjoy the life that it can produce for me because it can be converted into energy that can tremendously improve my life. I will never benefit from the law of combustion that God crafted when He designed the universe. If I don't realize that a life-changing truth exists and how it applies to me, I will never be able to take full advantage of it. If I don't understand the potential of my own mind,

I will never be able to take advantage of the almost limitless capacity God gave me when it comes to my mental faculties.

If I want to succeed in life, I must be told or I must discover for myself the vastness and the possibilities of all the principles God has woven into His creation, all the resources embedded within the elements. Then I must understand those laws and harness those resources and utilize them to my advantage. Until I understand the principles that hold the universe together and until I discover how to best apply those principles to my life, until I subdue my own mind and the other riches God has gifted to me and make those riches work to my benefit, they won't do me any good. They won't help me at all.

That is why I have written *Mindset Matters*. Most people do not know that their lives are a product of their thoughts, that their thinking shapes their choices and that their choices shape their lives. They don't see the connection between what goes on inside their heads and what goes on in the world around them. Instead, they simply float through life like Forrest Gump's feather in the wind, allowing themselves to be carried wherever the tides of life, the influences of their friends or their own immediate appetites happen to carry them. They follow the 96 percent.

There is a price to pay for success and happiness. The excellent things of life don't just fall into place for us simply because we were fortunate enough to be born. They are not guaranteed to anyone either by God, our parents or by any department of government. In the same way that a farmer must buy the seed and plant the seed before the land provides him with a yield, success awaits your choice of mental "seeds" before it will yield its bounty to you.

||||||||||||||||||||||||||||||||||||||||||||||||||||||||||||||||

UNTIL I UNDERSTAND THE PRINCIPLES THAT HOLD THE UNIVERSE TOGETHER AND UNTIL I DISCOVER HOW TO BEST APPLY THOSE PRINCIPLES TO MY LIFE, UNTIL I SUBDUE MY OWN MIND AND THE OTHER RICHES GOD HAS GIFTED TO ME AND MAKE THOSE RICHES WORK TO MY BENEFIT, THEY WON'T DO ME ANY GOOD.

We will discuss the price of success in the next chapter. But for now, understand that success begins with what you know. A man cannot achieve what he doesn't know or what he fails to understand. And few people understand the connection between their thinking and the quality of their lives. That is why few people succeed on an otherwise level playing field.

This sad fact is very strange indeed because, as I have explained, virtually every religion and every school of philosophical thought recognizes and appreciates the connection between a person's thinking and her destiny. From the beginning of time, the great and accomplished people of history have repeatedly proclaimed the fact that success finds its roots in the seeds of belief that we plant in our own minds. Yet for some reason, people have failed to get the message. They all start out on the road to success without even knowing how to get where they are going; therefore, many fall by the wayside and abandon their passions and desires in favor of mere survival.

CHAPTER 6

THE PRICE OF SUCCESS

In reading the lives of great men, I found that the first victory they won was over themselves . . . self-discipline with all of them came first.
—Harry S. Truman

W hen I was in school, many centuries ago, I remember studying Sir Isaac Newton (1642-1727). Specifically, I remember the laws of physics that Newton recognized and which he described in his writings. I recall from my studies how Newton's discoveries helped redefine science and helped shape man's understanding of the physical world. One of those laws I can still remember is Newton's third law of motion.

Newton's third law of motion simply states that when one body exerts a force on another body, the second body simultaneously exerts a force equal in magnitude and opposite in direction to that of the first body. In other words, for every action, there is an opposite and equal reaction.

This law is readily observable in the everyday physical processes that govern our universe. It is seen, for instance, when a person walks, pushing against the floor while the floor pushes back against the person, or in swimming when a person pushes back against the water while the water simultaneously pushes the person forward. Whenever an automobile travels down a highway, the tires push against the pavement and the pavement pushes back against the tires, causing forward motion for the car but erosion for the asphalt. Why does this happen? Because for every action there is an opposite and equal reaction!

This fixed principle of nature does not apply solely to the physical aspects of life; this law also applies to many of the unseen and non-physical parts of life. To jump in an upward direction, for example, you have to push downward with your legs against a solid foundation beneath your feet. To achieve your goals, you also have to push down against the realities that constrain you. Whether talking about physical momentum or life momentum, you cannot propel yourself upward without pushing downward or forward without pushing backward.

So your success in life will be directly proportional to the effort you exert toward the achievement of that success. The obstacles that you encounter in life are there to provide you with the forward momentum you need to achieve great things for yourself, but you must learn to push against these obstacles in order to gain momentum from them by utilizing the opposite force they were designed to create for you.

Earlier in this book, I quoted Jesus of Nazareth, who obviously had a lot of profound things to say during His short time on earth. Let me quote Jesus once more because He also had a lot to say about this particular subject. He said, for instance, "In this world you will have trouble" (John 16:33, NIV). He didn't sugarcoat it, and He didn't try to avoid it. He told His followers straight up that life would be diffi-cult at times. Life would not just "happen" for them simply because they were His followers. Instead, life would be filled with unwanted situations, challenging scenarios, and threatening circumstances that had the potential to rob these people of their destinies or deplete their potential to do the things God had called them to do.

But Jesus also told His followers that they could overcome all these things because He had overcome all these things (see the rest of John 16:33). This kind of excellence, however, would come at a high price. So Jesus taught each disciple to count the cost of completing his life's purpose before actually engaging that purpose and working to achieve it. He taught them that they should think about the price they would have to pay for success in their work for Him before they actually started that work.

|||||||||||||||||||||||||||||||||||||||||||||||||||||||||||||||||||||||

THE OBSTACLES THAT YOU ENCOUNTER IN LIFE ARE THERE TO PROVIDE YOU WITH THE FORWARD MOMENTUM YOU NEED TO ACHIEVE GREAT THINGS FOR YOURSELF, BUT YOU MUST LEARN TO PUSH AGAINST THESE OBSTACLES IN ORDER TO GAIN MOMENTUM FROM

"Don't begin until you count the cost," Jesus told His disciples (Luke 14:28, NLT). Anything worthwhile is readily available to the one who will embrace it and is willing to pay the price to attain it. But success never comes cheap. It isn't guaranteed. Success carries a high price tag. So even though all one hundred of our imaginary young people would tell you that they want to be successful in life, only four would actually follow through with that confession by doing the difficult things that are necessary to push against the natural barriers that stand between them and their goals. Four would actually thrust themselves forward toward the high calling that consumes their hearts by pushing back against the forces that obstruct their forward progress.

Every great achievement is protected by a high wall of hard work, sacrifice, risk, and delayed gratification. If you want to be a doctor, you had better be prepared to make excellent grades in high school, pay a lot of money to attend a top-notch college, be prepared to study your buns off, and pay even more money to attend medical school and launch a practice after graduation.

If you want to be a world-class athlete, you had better be prepared to go to bed early when all your friends are hanging out, get up early, eat the right kinds of food, avoid tobacco and alcohol, and work harder than all the would-be superstars who surround you every day at practice. You had better be prepared to develop a level of proficiency in your sport that is as close to perfection as possible.

Each person succeeds or fails according to his own capacity to visualize where he is going with his life, to force himself to do what is necessary to begin and complete his journey. While vision is the most important component of the success formula because it is the fountain from which success ultimately flows, vision alone won't guarantee success. Even when a strong vision consumes a person's heart, it is possible for that vision to wane if it is not nurtured—if the one who possesses it fails to pay the price that is required to bring it to life.

So what is the price we must pay as human beings to achieve our dreams and our goals? What is the cost of success? From my perspective and based on my experiences and observations, there are five mental costs associated with success. Remember, in the world of personal achievement, the costs of success are typically associated with delayed gratification exemplified through various expressions of self-control. So these are the five areas of mental self-control that are essential for the person who wants to break out of the rut of mediocrity and rise to a level of exceptionalism that distinguishes him from the 96 percent.

CONTROL YOUR THOUGHTS.

Because of the subject matter of *Mindset Matters*, it should come as no surprise that the first cost you must be willing to pay for personal and professional success is the cost of controlling your own thinking. Throughout this book, I have presented an airtight case for the proposition that a person's thinking shapes the outcome of that person's life. In my arguments, I have tried to show that a person becomes what she thinks and experiences in life what she continually thinks about. So in order to control the direction and destination of your life, it is absolutely essential that you learn to control your own thinking. What you ponder in your own head and the attitude with which you ponder it will have everything to do with the track that your life follows.

This means, of course, that you must decide where you want to go before you actually start traveling there, because, until you determine the harvest you would like to reap in the fall, you won't know what kinds of seeds you should plant in the springtime. If you want the outcome of your life to be the same for you as it is for the 96 percent who fail to achieve their goals, you won't need to worry very much about the kinds of seeds you should choose to plant in your mind. But if you want the outcome of your life to be exceptional, like the 4 percent who achieve success, you will need to start thinking right now in ways that are different from the masses. You will need to learn how to take control of your own mind and feed it with good stuff so that the good stuff you sow into your mind can produce a good harvest in your life at the appropriate time in the future.

Robert Terson, a writer and speaker who specializes in the art of salesmanship, explains that a person actually has two different "minds": the conscious mind and the subconscious mind. The subconscious mind, according to Terson, is the real control center of a person's life. And I agree.

"The subconscious mind is the computer-command-center of your being," Terson explains, "the subterranean regulator of your physical, mental, and emotional functioning. Think of it as a mainframe computer regulating the air conditioning, heating, lighting, elevators, et cetera, in a skyscraper; you can't see it, but it's there, running things."

Your subconscious mind, therefore, is the real power behind your life because your subconscious mind dictates the way you perceive the world around you and the way you approach every decision that you make. In short, it dictates every facet of your existence. Your subconscious mind, like the mainframe computer that Terson uses as the analogy, can only function in response to the data that is programmed into it. If you program a computer with bad data, it will give you bad results. And if you program your subconscious with bad data, it will give you bad thinking. If you program your subconscious with wisdom and insight, with wholesome aspirations and legitimate plans to make your life better, it will guide you through the darkness to the destination that you seek. Like the autopilot on a Boeing 747, it will take control of the entire aircraft and guide you safely through the storm to your predetermined destination.

"The default setting is Garbage In," Terson explains, "which is why it's so important for you to constantly stand guard over your thoughts and emotions. It's why you must feed your subconscious the healthy thoughts and emotions it needs to provide the positive support you'll continuously require to succeed. Indulge in negative thinking and emoting and you'll be your own worst enemy."

Have you ever heard the saying, "He who controls his mind controls his life"? Well, the reverse to that statement is just as true: He who doesn't control his mind doesn't control his life. The person who would push against the status quo in order to propel himself forward must learn the importance of controlling the thoughts that he thinks, the beliefs that he holds, the choices that he makes, the actions that he takes, the words that he speaks, the images that he allows to fill his head, and the emotions and attitudes that flow out of him through his words, deeds, and the way he relates to other people and the world around him. While the person who does a good job handling this responsibility is destined to do better in life than the person who doesn't, the person who does a poor job at this task is destined to succumb to the mediocrity that plagues the 96 percent. That person will fall short in his relationships, goals, and his pursuit of personal significance.

Let me give you a simple, real-life scenario to help you understand how our unhealthy thoughts can control our lives in detrimental ways. A woman decides she wants to have a quiet, intimate dinner with her husband. So during the summer months, while her children are out of school and visiting their grandparents, she plans a candle-light dinner for a Friday night at the end of her husband's busy work week. Her husband knows about his wife's special plans, and he has promised to be home by six o'clock to enjoy his favorite home-cooked meal with his bride of fifteen years.

However, as the hands on the clock reach 6:15, this woman's husband isn't home yet. Therefore, annoyance starts building in her mind. That's not good because she is unable to recognize the mental "triggers" that are taking her down a dark hole of vain imagination that is going to cause her a lot of unnecessary stress and possibly damage her relationship with her husband in the process. In reality, the annoyance that is growing inside this woman's mind has nothing to do with the circumstances that are unfolding around her. She isn't annoyed because her husband is fifteen minutes late; she is annoyed because his tardiness must mean something more substantive. It must mean that he is taking her for granted, he lied to her, he doesn't care about her as much as he used to, or something terrible has happened to him on his way home.

In reality, this woman's husband is stuck in Friday-afternoon traffic, traffic that is worse than usual due to a three-car pileup on the entrance ramp to the turnpike. And he hasn't called home yet to explain his tardiness because he typically turns off his phone before getting behind the wheel of his car. Yet this man's wife is driving herself into a deep frenzy and a deep sense of anger and agitation. She is slipping into this unnecessary mental free fall because she doesn't recognize how her subconscious mind is connecting unrelated dots to take her to an unrealistic place.

|||||||||||||||||||||||||||||||||||||||||||||||||||||||||||||||||||

WHEN YOU FAIL TO CONTROL YOUR THINKING, YOU CAN EASILY DO DAMAGE TO YOUR LIFE.

When your mind is saturated with preconceived notions based on false assumptions that flow from bad experiences in your past, you are not controlling your thinking. When you fail to control your thinking, you can easily do damage to your life. At the very least, you can create anxiety for yourself that is both harmful and unnecessary because the way you respond to people and to challenges when you are flustered is the way you will learn to deal with similar situations in the future.

So as Travis Robertson suggests (Robertson Coaching International), learn to stop your thoughts, especially the thoughts that are arousing negative emotions and responses, and identify the specific negative thought patterns affecting you. You can do this by working backward. Start with the emotion that is consuming you at the moment, and wade through all the psychological junk that is going on inside you until you uncover the specific thought that gave rise to that emotion because every feeling you have is a direct result of something you are thinking.

Then, once you have isolated the thought that gave rise to your unhealthy feeling, recognize the little "movie" that is looping inside your head so you can stop it and replace it with a more realistic scenario. When a current situation reminds us subconsciously of a previous situation that was painful in some way, we tend to replay that little video over and over in our minds, and the mind seems to be disposed toward the negative experiences of the past rather than the positive experiences we have had in life. Intentional disruption of that process, therefore, is often necessary until our minds are conditioned to think in more healthy ways.

CONTROL YOUR LIMITED THINKING.

Don't take this personally, but if you could honestly evaluate your own thought processes, you would probably find that you are more narrow-minded than you realize, at least in certain areas. How do I know? Because you are human, and human beings tend to be quite restricted in their creativity and capacity to change! We like to think of ourselves as unique individuals with unique concepts and unique approaches to life. In reality, however, few people ever venture very far from the familiarity of the world into which they were born. Few people tend to think in truly innovative ways.

Just recently a friend of mine was visiting his adult children and his grandchildren in another state, and he was telling me how they all sat down one evening to watch a movie together on his son's big-screen, high-definition television with surround sound. The movie was entitled *White House Down*, a political action thriller released in 2013. But my friend told me that the movie was almost a word-for-word and scene-for-scene remake of the 1988 classic, *Die Hard*. The names were different and the characters' roles were slightly changed. The surroundings were different and the music was updated a bit, but the plot was a dead-on duplicate of the 1988 film.

That is what I am talking about when I say that few of us tend to think in unique or creative ways. Most of today's top songs are rearrangements of old tunes. Top movies are modifications of blockbusters from yesteryear. Fashion is borrowed from the popular styles of the past. News is nothing more than recycled information. And most political ideas are initiatives that failed in the past, yet are being touted to a new generation of voters who are unaware of their ineffectiveness.

People just don't know how to color outside the lines, how to dig down deep and find something genuine that they can share with the human race. As mortal human beings, we are conditioned to say that we are open to change and innovation, that we want to grow personally. We are conditioned to recite the popular mantra that all of us are exceptional and that every individual is unique. In reality, however, we are often nothing more than replicas of those around us. If we were all truly unique in our thinking, 96 percent of us would not end up in the same wretched place.

If the opposite of creative thinking is limited thinking, how can we actually recognize limited thinking when it starts to raise its ugly head and intrude upon our lives? In their book, *Thoughts and Feelings: Taking Control of Your Moods and Life*, authors Matthew McKay, Martha Davis, and Patrick Fanning tell us that limited thinking manifests itself in at least eight ways. To avoid these eight common practices, therefore, is to avoid the pitfall of limited thinking that stymies so many people today and robs them of their potential.

"Overgeneralization" is a manifestation of limited thinking. People tend to draw broad, general conclusions based on isolated personal experiences or random pieces of "evidence." "Polarized reasoning" is another manifestation. It results when we look at things as black-and-white, with no room for shades of gray. "Filtering" causes us to focus on one aspect of a situation while mostly ignoring other contributing factors. And "mind-reading" is the very common practice of making snap judgments about other people without the benefit of all the facts.

The list continues. "Catastrophizing," according to these three writers, is the tendency to mentally remake every unpleasant situation into a potential catastrophe before it actually becomes one. It is the "doomsday" type of thinking that compels people to expect the worst from every situation in life. "Magnifying" is the practice of blowing things up in our minds so that we "magnify" a situation, emphasizing words or events beyond their actual relevance to the other facts. Then "personalization" is the mental habit of subconsciously testing one's own value by comparing oneself with others. And "shoulds" are pretty much self-explanatory. We destroy ourselves internally by constantly creating and enforcing inflexible and unattainable rules for ourselves that are completely impossible to satisfy.

So we do a lot of things to ourselves on a mental level that are not healthy or conducive to growth or success and are just downright destructive. The good news, though, believe it or not, is that these patterns of thinking can be interrupted and displaced if we will only start isolating them and working on them individually as I explained above.

God believed in the creativity and innovation of the human race when He first formed the man and the woman in the Garden of Eden. How do I know this? God simply told man to "subdue" the earth (see Genesis 1:28), and then God stepped aside and let Adam and Eve have at it. He didn't tell them what to look for, what to do with it when they found it, and why they needed to do it. Instead, He simply told them to "subdue" the earth, and then He allowed them to unleash the limitless potential of their own minds so they could explore the world's mysteries and harness the world's resources for the overall good of mankind.

And guess what happened? By the seventh generation, the human race had achieved phenomenal things. Because of his tendency to probe and explore and investigate and recreate the world, man had already become proficient in urbanization, agriculture, animal husbandry, and metallurgy. He had already become skillful, with no prodding from heaven above, in poetry and in music.

Man, even in his fallen and sinful state, is still a reflection of the God who created him. So man's potential is almost limitless when compared to his achievements thus far. The control center for all of man's creativity is his mind—the seat of his inventiveness and the core of his ingenuity. Man, created in the image and likeness of God, is meant to do more than simply follow the herd over the cliff into the bottomless abyss below. Man is meant to imagine things that have not yet taken shape so he can harness the resources of God's creation in an effort to bring those imaginations to life.

Let your mind soar as it was designed to do. Set it free. Loosen the fetters that restrain it, and remember that imagination is one of the truly wondrous things that separate man from the lower forms of life that live merely by biological instinct, not purposeful motivation. Let your mind ascend to new heights until you finally come to realize that most of your limitations are self-imposed, not naturally imposed, and that the opportunities available to you today are enormous beyond belief.

Don't let pettiness govern your interactions with others or prejudice shape your perception of those around you. Don't let self-centeredness, self-pity, or low self-esteem rob you of your ability to work with others to achieve great things. Don't let insecurity, vindictiveness, a lack of honesty or a scarcity of integrity brand you with a bad reputation. Learn to recognize and overcome overgeneralization, filtering, and all the other things your limited thinking will try to force upon you because you have the capacity to do anything you want to do within your designed scope of operation. If others have done great things in their assigned spheres, you can do great things in yours. Imagine it.

CONTROL YOUR NEGATIVE ATTITUDE.

Are you a person of faith? Whether you know it or not, you are a person of faith because most of what you do in life is done by faith. When you marry another person, you do it by faith. You don't know for sure what the future holds for your newfound relationship, but you enter that relationship anyway. You have faith that it will contribute to your happiness and to the personal fulfillment that you seek. When you take a job, you do it by faith. You don't have any guarantees that your new job will last forever or that it will be a positive experience for you professionally. You cannot see at the time how your professional goals might change in the future or how the company you have joined might change, as well. Nevertheless, you take that job in spite of all the uncertainties because you believe in your heart that it is the right thing for you at the time and for the people who hired you.

As human beings, we forge our relationships, make our investments, pursue our educations, and make every professional decision in our lives simply on the basis of faith. We buy houses, launch business ventures, and drive to work every morning with faith in our hearts that we will arrive at the office unscathed and return that same evening to our families. We believe that certain things are good for us, right for us, and will carry us toward the destiny that awaits us. We also believe that other things are harmful to us, and it is best to avoid those things as much as possible.

While we make so many of our decisions, not on the basis of statistical data or cold analytics, but rather on the basis of faith, the fact remains that we don't usually have any assurances that our beliefs will actually materialize, any guarantees that our choices will lead to the success we hope to attain. We simply have internal convictions and an invisible set of persuasions that certain portals to the future are beneficial for us and certain others aren't. We have faith.

So if most of life's major decisions are driven by faith instead of guarantees and if the odds are in your favor that good things will happen for you more frequently than not, what is it about human nature that leads us to anticipate the worst about virtually every challenge we face, almost every threatening situation we encounter?

In the previous section, I mentioned the common mental practice of "catastrophizing." Catastrophizing is simply a mental defense mechanism that we employ subconsciously in order to protect ourselves emotionally. In any situation where discomfort is a possibility and failure is a prospect, we tend to migrate in our minds toward a tragic or catastrophic outcome for that situation before it has a chance to unfold. We do this to prepare ourselves for possible disappointment, to subconsciously fortify our minds against any unpleasantries that might arise. By nature, therefore, we humans are negative in our thinking.

Just think about it! Your telephone rings at 3:00 a.m. Your primary care doctor leaves a message on your voicemail, telling you that she wants you to schedule a follow-up appointment as soon as possible to discuss your recent lab results. Your postal carrier rings your doorbell because she needs you to sign for a special delivery letter. What is the first thing that runs through your mind in each of these situations?

Any time a potentially painful situation arises in our lives, our minds instinctively go straight for the gutter and focus on the most cata-strophic outcome possible for that particular situation. They do this in order to psychologically prepare us for any emotional "jolt" that might be coming down the pike.

But this natural mental disposition can become crippling when a person allows it to go too far or to become the first response. When expectations of negativity start creeping into a person's dreams, imag-inations, goals and efforts to aggressively seize the future, that person has a real spiritual problem that is going to effectively neutralize any potential he might have to achieve the things that are embedded in his soul. When our minds migrate instantly and repetitively toward the most terrible possible outcome in every situation we face—even when there is no hard evidence to support such a conclusion—suc-cess in life will be difficult to grasp.

It seems, therefore, that the typical 21st-century human being is a mixed bag of psychological contradictions. The typical person these days seems to enter marriage without giving it a great deal of thought, registers for college without a clear plan for what to study, and accepts job offers without fully contemplating how those decisions might add to or detract from personal and professional goals. Ironically, when a potential problem arises, that same person will typically go straight to the gutter in his or her expectations regarding the outcome of that situation.

Unfortunately, this is the opposite of the way successful people approach life. Successful people approach all their major decisions with guarded optimism. They approach marriage, for instance, with their minds as well as their hearts. They pursue their educations with a clear understanding of how each academic step might contribute to their long-term goals. And they only accept job offers that can help them achieve their professional ambitions, and then only after researching the company, the broader industry, and the future prospects for that particular segment of the economy.

When problems arise, they don't wallow in despair like the 96 percent. They don't fret and worry and wring their hands in anxious anticipation of terrible news because they have already prepared themselves for any unpleasant eventualities that might occur. They've readied a "lifeboat" and a "survival kit" that can actually help them navigate troubled waters and help them prosper while the people around them are trying to recover from the destruction. They see catastrophe, therefore, not as the end to their dreams, but as a new opportunity to expand their dreams and make forward progress at a much faster pace.

While successful people are more prepared for danger than those around them and realize that certain challenges are unavoidable in life, successful people don't live in the expectation of a worst-case scenario for life's unpleasant experiences. They understand that a few unwanted events are bound to occur over the course of a lifetime, that the false expectation of catastrophe is often more destructive than the challenge itself. It can create all kinds of physical, financial, mental, and relational damage that real events won't. Besides, most of our fears never turn into real events anyway, and they never do the damage that they threaten to do. Perhaps Mark Twain summarized it best when he said, "I've had a lot of worries in my life, most of which never happened."

Keep in mind that there is a greater mathematical probability that tomorrow's weather will be sunny rather than rainy and you will live to life expectancy instead of dying young. But if you are "average" in your thinking and tomorrow is your wedding day, you will probably worry about rain. And if a strange and inexplicable pain seems to linger in your rib cage, you will probably start searching the internet for statistics related to lung cancer.

There is just something about the human psyche that steers us straight toward the pit in our expectations regarding future events. When it comes to life in general, we tend to take life for granted, assuming that everything will work out for the best. But when it comes to our specific challenges, we tend to rehash those challenges over and over in our minds until we have written a completely fabricated script of utter doom for ourselves.

||||||||||||||||||||||||||||||||||||||||||||||||||||||||||||||||||

THERE IS JUST SOMETHING ABOUT THE HUMAN PSYCHE THAT STEERS US STRAIGHT TOWARD THE PIT IN OUR EXPECTATIONS REGARDING FUTURE EVENTS.

This is why most people spend a lot of their time whining, complaining and criticizing others for their plight in life. They blame their wives, husbands, parents, and children. They blame their bosses, pastors, neighbors, and the government. If something goes wrong for them, somebody else must have caused it to happen. Even God is susceptible to their faultfinding. The people who get ahead in life take responsibility for their lives and think positively about their own potential in order to bring good conclusions to their challenges and good outcomes to their opportunities.

Therefore, learn to concentrate on all the good things in your life. Develop a positive attitude regarding the future outcome of your challenges because most of the fears you have had in your life never turned into realities anyway and most of the fears you have right now will never happen either. So regardless of what you may be facing, face it with courage and do it with hope because this, too, will probably turn out for your benefit.

Obviously, life is not smooth sailing all the time. If it were, everybody would be successful without effort. Life is more like an obstacle course, designed to separate the weak from the strong, the focused from the wishy-washy. Don't look at your obstacles as tragedies; look at them as opportunities to set yourself apart from the field, to prove your mettle and to showcase your abilities. In the end, out of the one hundred people who start the journey, only four will finish and only one will do it with style. Expect some impediments to interfere with your forward progress. And when they do, look beyond them with a positive disposition. Then, climb over them, run around them, or, if necessary, dig a tunnel underneath them. One way or the other, get through those impediments because you know that you can.

When you have a clearly defined goal for your life and your eyes are fixed on the prize that awaits you at the finish line, it is easier to think positively about the future, even when the present is filled with complications. Remember, therefore, that your mental state and your outlook are everything when you encounter the kinds of tests that can make the race more difficult.

One enduring truth is that there is no such thing as a problem without a solution. Let me repeat that! There is no such thing as a problem without a solution. Let your imagination freely explore the various solutions that may be available to you whenever you face a trial. Usually, there is more than one solution to even the most difficult conundrums in life. Then make up your mind which solution you want to implement, and get busy attacking the problem. That is the formula for success—for overcoming adversity.

Again, it's all about your belief systems (faith) and your vision. If a worthy ambition drives you, you will be willing to pay the price that is associated with solving any problem that stands between you and your dream, and you will believe in your ability to pay that price and to produce the outcome you are seeking. You are not "most people," so constantly remind yourself that, regardless of what is happening around you, a good outcome is more likely than a bad one. Even if the situation produces a temporary problem, that problem can't defeat you. It can only force you to deal with it. When your objective is clear in your own heart and mind, you will deal with it decisively.

CONTROL YOUR TENDENCY TO WASTE RESOURCES.

You have been endowed with many excellent and worthwhile tools that are designed to fuel your march toward success. Among these valuable commodities are your time, money, talents, relationships, and opportunities. Even though you possess all these good things in abundance, you do not possess them without measure. All are finite and must be managed carefully.

When it comes to the great treasures of life, there are two mistakes that people usually make. Most people either waste life's precious resources by spending them unwisely while disregarding the future, or they hoard these things in fear, never utilizing them to enhance their lives. The mystical thing about life's treasures is that they are worthless unless they are "spent." To hoard them is to make them ineffective and worthless, but to use them hastily and without a plan is to extinguish them altogether without an adequate return on your investment.

Successful people think of their time, money, talents, relationships, and opportunities as resources to be used and treasures to be invested wisely in the hope of a greater return. That is why successful people make sacrifices today in order to reap benefits tomorrow. They say "no" to their appetites right now with the expectation of feasting tomorrow on the bounty that their resources produce.

Consider talent. If you would be completely honest with yourself and not be swayed by pride on the one hand or timidity on the other, you would have to admit that you possess a few talents that have the capacity to set you apart from the crowd. Perhaps your talents lie in art, music, your genuine fondness for children, your ability to grasp mathematical concepts, or your ability to build things with your hands. Every human being has at least one talent that has the potential to set that person apart and equip him or her for success in life.

But talents are a lot like the raw resources that God placed in the physical creation. We have to find, extract, harness, and perfect them. We have to develop them and discover their full potential. Few people seem willing to do that. Talent in music may be given by God, but that talent must be nurtured and honed by the individual who possesses it. A talent that is not sharpened and refined through training, practice, use, and strengthening is a talent that will basically produce nothing for the one who possesses it.

Or let's consider the role that money plays in our lives. Most people live above their means and are in debt up to their eyebrows, barely surviving from paycheck to paycheck and from crisis to crisis. That is why most people have no savings and no investments. But most of the self-made millionaires among us (according to *USA Today*, there are 5,200,000 millionaire households in the United States) are people who chose to live below their means early in life so they could save and invest a sensible portion of what their hands produced. Then, over time, those investments grew, and now their futures look bright.

If a young man starting his first job out of college at the age of twenty-three would resolve to drive a used car instead of going into debt to buy a new car and would share a three-bedroom house with two other recent college graduates instead of leasing an upscale apartment in a swank neighborhood, and if he would start the practice of saving just 10 percent of his income every week, investing it sensibly and steadily in sound financial vehicles over the course of his life, that young man would be a self-made, independent millionaire by the time he reached the age of forty. That's not my opinion; that is a mathematical fact. Then he could keep working, using that large stash of money to produce even more money for himself and his family. And by the time he finally reached retirement age, he would have enough to live comfortably for the rest of his life with an impressive amount left over for his children, grandchildren, and all the charitable causes he would like to enrich.

The difference is self-discipline, self-denial that flows from a vision, delayed gratification motivated by a dream and driven by a plan. The difference is a conscious refusal to follow the herd and instead take a different path in life.

The 96 percent who are wasteful don't just waste their money; they waste other resources that are far more valuable. Don't get me wrong; money is important. But money is probably the least valuable of the gifts we possess. It can be replaced when it is lost or stolen. Truly irreplaceable commodities, like time and opportunity, cannot be replaced. And sadly, most people waste these precious resources as quickly and thoughtlessly as they waste their hard-earned cash.

Not every human being is equal in talent and wealth, but every human being is given the same amount of time in a day and the same number of days in a year. Every human being will have a limited number of life-changing opportunities during the time that person spends on this earth. It's what we choose to do with our limited reserves—our God-given resources—that determines whether we end up in the company of the 4 percent or the swollen ranks of the 96 percent.

Great people make good use of their time, just as they make good use of their money. They don't waste the most precious resources God has entrusted to them. Yes, they spend the vast majority of their time doing the necessary things that all of us do to stay alive and to function in the real world. They eat, sleep, work, and spend a reasonable amount of time relaxing and enjoying their lives. But successful people know that the difference between greatness and mediocrity is what they choose to do with that little bit of spare time that most of us waste without thinking about it. While most people hurry home after work so they can play video games all night or sit in front of the television until their eyelids become so heavy they have to be carried to bed, the people who end up changing the world are those who squeeze the life out of time. They make good use of the time that most people squander.

Did you know that if you would invest just fifteen minutes a day in some worthwhile pursuit, you could become an expert in that discipline within a couple of years? That's right! Just using your spare time, you could turn your world upside down in just two or three years. The Dell Computer Corporation was established in a dormitory room at the University of Texas, and Facebook was started by a student at Harvard University. Amazon and Google were both launched out of garages, and Nordstrom was founded by a sixteen-year-old immigrant from Sweden who picked potatoes for a living after arriving in the United States, not knowing a word of English and with just $5 in his pocket. These visionaries were willing to work on their ideas between classes, to push their dreams forward a little each day after putting in a full day of labor at a job that was personally unfulfilling.

It's not just time that matters. As I have explained, money matters too because money is really nothing more than the currency you are willing to accept as a replacement for your valuable time. What do you do with the currency you have exchanged for your time? Do you spend all of it and then borrow a little more each month just to maintain your lifestyle, or do you live slightly beneath your means so you can save and invest some of your money for a future cause? What do you do with your spare time, those "extra" hours each week you are not spending to earn a living? After you have put in your time at your place of work, taken care of the necessities of life, and allowed yourself some reasonable "downtime," what do you do with all that remains? Do you waste it on meaningless activities that are intended to occupy your idle mind or invest it with the hope of producing more wealth and more independence for yourself? Do you use your spare time wisely by investing it in your health and your relationships, or do you just sit on the dock of the bay watching the tide roll away?

What about those precious relationships that give your life its true meaning? Do you spend the majority of your time with people who are doing nothing and going nowhere with their lives? Or do you seek to nurture relationships with people who are aggressively pursuing greatness, people who have lofty goals for themselves and who possess the kind of values that are worthy of their goals?

Relationships are one of life's commodities that we often fail to consider, but relationships, arguably more important than time or money, are important for two big reasons. First, relationships have an eternal value whereas time as we know it will end, and money, as we know it, will eventually become meaningless. Relationships have an eternal value. Your life will affect those who come after you—your children and grandchildren—in more ways than you might imagine. You will have a lasting impact on the friends who survive you, on the community and the company you helped shape, and on the people you touched over the course of your life. Your words will linger, your influence will continue to shape people after you are gone, your genetics will be perpetuated through your offspring, and your earthly possessions will be handed off to others who have the potential to benefit from them.

But your relationships have a second intrinsic value that you may never have contemplated. Even if you have ignored your relationships in the past, you are destined to learn that your relationships are actually the most precious things you possess in life because, as you grow older and the end of your life starts drawing near, you won't worry about that yacht you were never able to buy, that big mansion you were never able to build in the Bellaire subdivision. You won't fret over the fact that you never broke par on the golf course or that you never managed to win the "salesman of the year" award at your company. When the end of your time on earth draws near, all your attention will be turned toward those you have loved. You will care about your relationship with God. You will care about the husband or wife who has stood by your side for decades, your children and your grandchildren, all the friends you have made over the course of your life, and the people who have given your life its true meaning and filled it with joy.

Consequently, if relationships are that important and if relationships with other successful people can help you attain your goals, shouldn't your relationships be a major focus in your life right now? Shouldn't they be more than just peripheral annoyances that require more of your time than you are willing to give? Of course, they should! Relationships not only make life worth living; good relationships make life fulfilling. They help make life spiritually, emotionally, financially and professionally successful. You are the byproduct of the network of people you have chosen to build around yourself.

And then there's opportunity. Regardless of your status in life or your age or where you came from or where you currently live, opportunities will present themselves for you to advance. What do you plan to do with these occasional passages to a better future? The vast majority of the people (about 96 percent) can't even recognize an opportunity when it comes knocking on their door because it always puts on a disguise before it rings the doorbell. It looks like hard work or risk. And since most people despise risk and avoid unnecessary work, people tend to turn down their opportunities instead of inviting them into their lives. Most people miss doing something really great with their lives because they are afraid of the price they must pay or the risks they must take in order to pursue those opportunities.

What you choose to do with your money, time, relationships, talents, and your opportunities when they come knocking on your door will determine where you end up in life. Sure, nobody gets it right every time. All of us waste our precious resources from time to time. But when your days on earth are extinguished and you have finished your assigned course, your place in the ranks of the finishers will be determined by the combined effect of the choices you have made regarding how you should spend the limited resources God has placed in your hands. If you made mostly good choices based on sound reasoning and wisdom, your name will appear close to the top of the leaderboard. But if you made mostly poor choices based on shortsightedness and your own immediate comforts, your name will appear with the also-rans in the small print at the bottom of the page. You are free to choose, but the danger inherent in freedom is that you always have the God-given right to make the wrong choice.

||||||||||||||||||||||||||||||||||||||||||||||||||||||||||||||||

WHAT YOU CHOOSE TO DO WITH YOUR MONEY, TIME, RELATIONSHIPS, TALENTS, AND YOUR OPPORTUNITIES WHEN THEY COME KNOCKING ON YOUR DOOR WILL DETERMINE WHERE YOU END UP IN LIFE.

CONTROL YOUR TENDENCY TO BE MENTALLY LAZY.

Ideas are worthless unless we act on them. Accumulate all the wisdom and knowledge you can possibly gather, gain all the experience you can possibly acquire, and do all the planning and testing of your hypotheses that you can possibly do before you raise anchor and set sail for the promised land. Without direction and without preparation, you are doomed to fail on your quest for the golden fleece.

After you have done your due diligence to prepare yourself for the pursuit of your life's vision, get up, put on your sailor suit, and start hoisting the sails and swabbing the decks because you'll never actually get where you are going until your plans turn into actions. Eventually, you will have to stop talking because talk is cheap. You will have to stop planning because no plan can ever be perfect. At some point, you will have to just trust God, yourself, your vision, and your blueprint for fulfilling your vision. Eventually, you will have to take your first step and start rowing your boat toward a distant shore.

One of the most notable distinctions between doers and dreamers is that doers eventually *do* while dreamers never stop talking about what they *intend* to do. We like to talk a big talk, but when it comes time to step into the public arena and show people what we are really made of, that possibility frightens most of us and drives us into a perpetual state of inactivity. You need to work, therefore, to overcome this human tendency. Start doing something today to fulfill your vision for life, even if it's just a tiny step forward.

Anna Chui, a writer who imparts a lot of helpful information about life, tells the story of two grains that were lying side by side on some fertile soil. The first grain said to the second grain, "I want to grow up. I want to put down roots deep in the ground and sprout from the soil. I dream of blossoming into delicate buds that proclaim the coming of spring. I want to feel the warm rays of the sun and the cool dew drops on my petals."

So this grain grew up and became strong and fruitful.

Then the second grain said, "I'm afraid. If I put down roots in the soil, I don't know what they will face there. If I grow tender shoots, they might be damaged by the wind. And if I eventually make flowers, they might wither and die after some time. So I think I'm going to contemplate this whole thing a little longer—put my dreams on hold and wait for a safer time."

But while the second grain was waiting for the perfect time to start pursuing its destiny, a chicken passed by and pecked it. So much for that little grain's ambitions!

If you want to eventually get to a great place in life, you are going to have to take some small steps every day to get there. And if you do, you will eventually arrive. This thought, by the way, brings me back to Sir Isaac Newton and another one of his fixed laws of physics. Newton's first law of motion states that "a body at rest stays at rest and a body in motion stays in motion unless acted upon by an external force." That is why the world's movers and shakers are prone to action, not thinking. They would rather do something today and make a course correction tomorrow than spend their whole lives thinking about what they want to do and watching others get there ahead of them. So make yourself take steps toward your destiny each day. Make yourself move forward in life, starting now. It is hard to move a boulder, but once you get it rolling, it is even harder to stop it.

In conclusion, let's get real. Common sense tells us that the most successful people aren't always the smartest people because the smartest kids in school don't always succeed in the real world. Experience tells us that they aren't always the most talented people because a lot of people with talent never figure out how to turn their talents into gold. In addition, hard work doesn't seem to be the magic key to success, at least not by itself because a lot of people work long hours and come home tired at the end of the day, yet they never manage to achieve their dreams or pursue their deepest ambitions.

The common thread that runs through the lives of the world's most accomplished people is the vision that drives them, but without a resulting work ethic, exemplified by a willingness to pay the price for achieving that vision, the vision is bound to die. In fact, a vision can actually become a source of frustration and inner shame if it is not accompanied by an effort to bring it to life. A vision unfulfilled is in many ways worse than no vision at all.

Understand, therefore, that a personal vision is both a blessing and a curse. It is a blessing in the sense that it is the most vital ingredient for success. To have a real vision that drives you toward your life's purpose is to be set apart from most of the people around you. But a vision can be a curse in the sense that it requires a lot from the one who possesses it.

An inner motivation toward a purposeful life may be a free gift from God, but it is a gift that requires maintenance by the one who possesses it. A vision will cost you in a lot of ways, especially early on. But as you make the necessary investments and pay the necessary price to bring your vision to fulfillment and as you reap the rewards that flow from your vision after it finally starts to mature, you will find that your return on investment is rich indeed and that the personal satisfaction you derive from your achievements is worth more than any price you could ever be required to pay.

CHAPTER 7

THE PROOF IS IN
THE PUDDING

*Don't fear failure so much that you refuse to try new
things. The saddest summary of a life contains three
descriptions: could have, might have, and should have.*
—Louis E. Boone

N ot long ago, I was at breakfast with a friend of mine, and he told me that he and his wife were planning to start a gluten-free diet. I don't know a lot about nutrition, so I don't understand all the intricacies involved with eating gluten-free. But my friend was telling me that he and his wife had been experiencing some stomach problems and that a physical therapist had recommended they try eating gluten-free and dairy-free for fourteen straight days to see if those dietary changes might help them. Apparently, my friend was in the middle of buying the necessary foods when we met for breakfast; he was planning to start the fourteen-day trial on Monday of the following week.

But now that his experiment is over, it seems that the gluten-free diet didn't help my friend very much. The diet did produce some positive results for his wife, however. In her early efforts to learn how the diet worked, she made a few mistakes and had to start over with her fourteen-day trial. But eventually, she managed to string together fourteen consecutive days of gluten-free and dairy-free eating, and some of the stomach problems she was having seemed to improve. Now another member of their family is getting ready to try the same diet to see if the experiment will work for him.

When we met for breakfast that day, my friend told me that he didn't think the gluten-free diet would help him very much, and he eventually proved to be right. Although his stomach problems were minor compared to those his wife was having, he didn't think his problem was related to wheat, barley, or rye. But knowing that millions of Americans are gluten intolerant, he thought the fourteen-day test was worthy of a try. After all, because he would be eating a healthier diet during those two weeks, he thought he might actually find some new foods he would like. So in his estimation, my friend had nothing to lose and much to gain. And that is why I want to encourage you to try the things I have been sharing with you in this book: You have nothing to lose, but everything to gain.

When most people see a book on the shelf, they usually just pass by and leave it there. Only a small number of people will pick it up and look through it. Among those who look, only a few will ever buy it. Likewise, among those who buy, only a few will ever read it. Most who read will soon forget what they have read. Fortunately, there is one category of people who will get a lot out of a good book and possibly be changed by the things they have read. The people who will actually benefit are the people who immediately put into action the things they have learned from that book.

For this reason, I am asking you to do more than simply read this book: I am asking you to *try* this book. For a short period of time, I want you to put the knowledge I have shared with you to work in your everyday life so you can experience firsthand just how powerful your own thought processes can be and how strongly your thinking can affect every aspect of your life. After all, unless you try the things you have learned, how can you know for sure if they really work? So let me tell you how you can test the things you have learned and how you can know with certainty that they have the power to alter your direction in life.

Every person, if he will search his heart and be completely honest with himself, will find that there is one thing deeply embedded in his soul that he wants more than anything else in life. That one thing, though sometimes hidden beneath a pile of personal fears and self-doubts, is the driving motivation of that person's life. It is one's destiny. So I want you to identify this primary driving motivation in your life—that one thing that floats your boat and quivers your liver more than anything else—and write it down in one phrase or one sentence so you can use it as a launching pad for a short-term trial of the things I have been sharing with you.

||||||||||||||||||||||||||||||||||||||||||||||||||||||||||||||||||||

EVERY PERSON, IF HE WILL SEARCH HIS HEART AND BE COMPLETELY HONEST WITH HIMSELF, WILL FIND THAT THERE IS ONE THING DEEPLY EMBEDDED IN HIS SOUL THAT HE WANTS MORE THAN ANYTHING ELSE IN LIFE.

Your focus statement doesn't have to concentrate on money. Maybe your focus statement should bypass money altogether and go straight to a goal you want to achieve with your money. For example, perhaps you want to build a house in a particularly nice neighborhood you have admired all your life, or you want to own a horse ranch in the country where there is lots of open space. If so, that should be your goal.

Perhaps your enticement in life isn't financial or material at all. Maybe you want to acquire a certain position in your company or be the highest producer in your field of labor even if it means a lower salary. Maybe you want to have the happiest and healthiest family possible, write a book, record a musical album, or do something benevolent to make an impact on humanity and leave a mark upon the world.

If you could achieve only one big thing before you die, what is it that you would like to achieve? Write it down, and then edit it. After that, edit it some more before you begin this test so your statement will accurately reflect the strongest motivation of your soul. Be specific. Don't write something vague like, "I want to be a good person" or "I want to be successful." Be precise, so you know exactly what you are striving for and how you can know when you have achieved it. Then set aside some time—at least four weeks—to carry your statement around with you so you can begin to make that goal the centerpiece of your thoughts.

I suggest a minimum of four weeks for your test because this trial run is designed to alter your thinking, and anything less than four weeks would not be enough time to create the kinds of changes you need. So find the soonest four-week block of time that you could dedicate to the test I am about to describe to you. Maybe this Sunday (the first day of the week) could work for you, or next Monday (the first day of the workweek)! Then mark off the next four weeks so those dates can be dedicated to completing your test. Or maybe you would like to do this for a whole month. Perhaps it would be easier for you to start this test on the first day of the upcoming month and then faithfully follow through with the test until the last day of the month (28-31 days).

It's up to you. It doesn't really matter when you start and when you stop. The thing that matters is that you take the test and complete the test as soon as possible, giving yourself at least four weeks to see if the information I have shared with you in this book can have a lasting effect on your life. And the good news is that the test is easy. It's not like a diet or anything that is designed to intrude upon your life. I'm not asking you to rearrange your daily schedule or to do something that is complicated or inconvenient. And I'm not asking you to alter your lifestyle in any discernible way. This test will only involve a slight modification in your behavior. But knowing in advance that it will only require a few weeks of your time, you should be able to easily fulfill your commitment to test my hypotheses for yourself.

Each morning, when you wake up, take that little card and read it a few times before you do anything else. Begin your day by thinking about that goal, and when you go to bed at night, read that card several times right before you turn out the lights, making your goal the last thing you see and the last thing you think about before you go to sleep.

Throughout the day, find opportunities to pull that little card out of your pocket or your purse and read it to yourself a few times. Read it before lunch and after lunch. Read it before going into your weekly staff meeting and after the meeting is over. Read it here, there, and every-where in between—while you are stuck in traffic or in an elevator. Just read it, read it, read it. The purpose of this exercise is to see how that one deliberate change in your thinking can start to change your entire life.

But here's the caveat: You have to see the test through to its comple-tion. You can't do the test on Monday and then skip it on Tuesday because Tuesday is your big meeting day. You can't do it Wednesday, Thursday, and Friday, and then forget about it over the weekend because you're planning to play golf with a friend who is visiting from out of town. You have to do this exercise faithfully every day for the duration of the dedicated time period. And if you don't, you have to start over until you fulfill this obligation for at least twenty-eight days in a row.

In *Mindset Matters*, I have quoted the Bible several times since it has heavily influenced the American culture since our nation's origins in the 17th century. Even if you don't personally embrace the Bible's teachings, the culture that has shaped you has been shaped itself by the teachings of the Bible. And in the Bible, there is an interesting parallel to this little test that I want you to consider before starting your own trial.

God wanted to change the thinking of the Jewish people. For four hundred years, the Jews had been slaves in Egypt. They had lived under Egyptian rule, been marinated in Egyptian culture, and been controlled by their Egyptian slave masters. Not a single Jew living at that time knew what it was like to think in any way except the Egyptian way. Not one knew what it meant to be free.

So when God led His people out of Egypt and when He was preparing to take them into their own land where they were destined to establish their own culture and sovereign nation, He gave them a set of laws and principles to adopt as the foundation of their own enduring culture. After giving these laws, God said to them, "Impress them on your children. Talk about them when you sit at home and when you walk along the road, when you lie down and when you get up. Tie them as symbols on your hands and bind them on your foreheads. Write them on the doorframes of your houses and on your gates" (Deuteronomy 6:7-9, NIV).

In other words, God knew about the potential of a person's thought life before any researchers had discovered it. And God should understand the potential of the human mind because God was the designer and creator of the brain. Consequently, since God understands the potential of the mind, as well as its vulnerabilities, He wanted His people to keep His laws in the forefront of their thinking so they could achieve with their lives every good thing God had created them to achieve.

That is why God instructed His people to think about His laws morning, noon, and night. He wanted them to rise in the morning, thinking about His laws, meditate on His laws throughout the day, and consider His laws one final time before going to bed at night. God wanted them to be on the lips of the people, in their hearts, and in their minds so they could absorb and follow them without undue effort. Knowing that people become what they think about, God wanted His people to think about Him and the power of His unchanging truths. He wanted them to ponder these truths constantly.

So I want you to do the same thing. While God asked the Jewish people to consider all of His laws every day of their lives, I'm asking you to consider just one thing for about a month. Then if this new practice works for you, you can keep doing it for the rest of your life. If it doesn't work for you, you'll find out, just like my friend found out that gluten-free eating doesn't help his digestive problems.

God understood what we now understand as a result of years of research. Without even realizing it, a person becomes what she thinks. She drifts toward those things. This test is designed to help you take the initial steps toward changing your thinking, to teach you to think—not about your fears or the negative things that might happen to you in the future, but about your strongest dream and the possibilities that await you—to help you learn how to focus on your purpose in life and how to mind your head so you can achieve that purpose. My expectation, if you do this test faithfully, is that you will soon realize that your greatest dream can actually be more than just a dream. It can become a reality, and you will begin to see ways that you can make it a reality as you dwell on it during your test period.

We all know that the earth is filled with abundance. Abundance is all around us. Especially in the most prosperous nation on earth, the abundance associated with prosperity is quite evident. In the past, therefore, you probably haven't noticed all that abundance on a conscious level because it has become so familiar to you. It has been part of your everyday experience. Beautiful homes! Luxurious cars! Elegant shops with fine works of art! Manicured lawns! Impressive, high-rise office buildings! Stone structures with large columns! You name it! You have been surrounded by this kind of thing all your life, so you have grown accustomed to it and are not the least bit enamored by its presence or its grandeur.

If prosperity becomes part of your dream, you will begin to see all that luxury and wealth in a different way as you ponder your goal and the possibilities of achieving it start to take shape in your imagination. You will begin to understand your own capacity to create wealth for yourself, see your own potential for sharing in the world's abundance. After all, you have as much right to the finer things in life as anyone else. But you have to start thinking like the 4 percent before you can ever hope to attain those finer things.

Fully understand my intentions here: I want you to learn a new habit, a habit that will undoubtedly be difficult at first but will become entrenched in your life as you discipline yourself to perform this new mental behavior for at least four weeks. If you will make yourself do the things that I have asked you to do for at least twenty-eight consecutive days and be consistent in your efforts, never wavering and never skipping a day, I promise you that you will have a new habit that will completely revolutionize you as a person and set you on a course that can alter the outcome of your life.

The goal of this test, therefore, is to help you stop thinking like everyone around you—narrowly and short-term. Stop thinking in limited ways about yourself and your potential in life. Start catching yourself every time you start drowning in the mundane and repetitive problems of day-to-day life that deplete all of a person's thinking time, leaving no time to consider nobler things. In a nutshell, I want you to learn to formulate a mental picture of your strongest personal goal so it can begin to dominate your thinking, impact your planning, alter your actions, and change your life.

Let me warn you in advance that there will be times when you will feel like quitting and going back to your old ways. It's not easy to learn a new behavior, especially when the old behavior is so deeply ingrained in your psyche. Hang in there; don't quit. You started thinking the way that you currently think before you could even walk or talk. You started seeing the world the way that you currently see it when you were just a little child, when your parents and the other significant adults in your life were shaping your developing mind with their own perceptions of the world and expectations of life. It took you all those years to learn to think the way that you think right now and to behave the way that you behave right now. So expect some time to pass before you can "unlearn" these old patterns and start replacing them with a whole new approach to living.

The good news is that you're never too old to learn something new. However, the longer you wait, the harder it will be. So get busy. Write down your personal vision and then set a date so you can get started with your test as soon as possible. This is an opportunity for you to resurrect your march toward the things you stopped thinking about years ago when you surrendered to the mindset of those around you and convinced yourself that your goals were too lofty to achieve. This is an opportunity for you to start thinking like that tiny group of people which has learned to visualize all the great possibilities of life rather than the difficulties associated with attaining them.

YOU'RE NEVER TOO OLD TO LEARN SOMETHING NEW. HOWEVER, THE LONGER YOU WAIT, THE HARDER IT WILL BE.

If you want to finally leave behind the world of unexceptional achievement and start living where the successful people do, you are going to have to start placing yourself in the company of those people right now by learning to think the way that they think. You can start this process by learning to take control of your own mind because it is the control center of your life. Let it only think about the things that you teach it to think about and only consider the data that you program into it.

During your month-long test, there are three specific things I want you to do as you glance throughout the day at your little index card and think about your primary goal in life.

1) THINK AS LITTLE AS POSSIBLE ABOUT THE PROBLEMS OF YOUR EVERYDAY LIFE. THINK AS MUCH AS POSSIBLE ABOUT THE GREATER GOAL THAT IS WRITTEN ON YOUR CARD.

Life is not going to stand still during your test. You will still have bills to pay and meet deadlines and responsibilities at work. You will still have disagreements with your spouse and issues with your kids. Taxes will come due, the tires will need replacing, and your heat pump will have to be serviced. That's life. But as much as possible, don't worry about these things or fret over them. Just take care of them and then get back to your little card. Saturate your mind with the possibilities of tomorrow, not the never-ending responsibilities of today.

Obviously, if something "big" happens—you need emergency surgery or a hurricane rolls through town and your house is seriously damaged—you may need to suspend this test for a while and start over at a later time. But I don't want you to let the customary, predictable, routine problems of life deter you from saturating your mind with the words on your card. In fact, the primary purpose of this test is to help you develop the habit of thinking about grander things in the midst of all the little things that usually consume your mental energy.

As with other subjects related to real life, Jesus said something very interesting about this subject, as well. In a parable about the different things that tend to rob us of our spiritual potential, Jesus used that old, familiar illustration of a seed. "A farmer went out to sow his seed,"

Jesus said in Matthew 13:3-7 (NIV). "As he was scattering his seed, some fell . . . among thorns, which grew up and choked the plants."

Later, Jesus explained this parable to his disciples. He said that the seed which fell among the thorns was illustrative of the person whose spiritual life is choked and made ineffective by "the worries of this life" (Matthew 13:22, NIV). Even back then, at a time when life was a lot simpler and much less stressful than it is today, Jesus realized that one of the greatest deterrents to personal and spiritual success is the constant intrusion of life's everyday concerns.

Most of us are so busy putting out the little "fires" that erupt around us every day, we never seem to have time for the things that matter most. The "tyranny of the urgent" makes it impossible for us to focus on the things that actually give life its meaning. Every day, there is a problem over here that needs immediate attention, one over there that needs a solution right away, a problem with a coworker, an invoice, the insurance company, or with an order that has to be returned. If we aren't careful, we can allow our whole lives to be consumed by nothing nobler than tending to all these little distractions.

I don't know if anybody has done any research on this subject, but I would venture to guess that the typical American today spends as much as half of his or her time fixing things that were working fine yesterday or fixing little problems that just seemed to suddenly appear out of nowhere. In fact, if you think about it, you could summarize most people's job descriptions in one simple sentence: "Your job is to fix problems for your boss."

Just think about it! Even if your job is something as simple as tightening a lug nut on a piece of machinery as it makes its way down an assembly line, that is a problem your boss doesn't want to fix. He has problems of his own to fix: tardy employees, payroll reports, next week's work schedule, and finding a replacement for the machinist who just quit. So he pays you money to take care of the lug nut for him, and his boss pays him money to take care of the payroll reports and the work schedule.

But before you can even focus on tightening that lug nut, you will have to deal with all the lesser problems that will arise to obstruct your efforts to solve the lug nut problem. In a typical hour on an assembly line, for instance, you might cut your hand and have to get it bandaged, drop your wrench and have to retrieve it from the tight spot beneath the machinery where it is really hard to reach, or clean up a small puddle of oil that you spilled in your work area.

I think you get the point. Even while you are solving problems, you have to take breaks from solving those problems so you can solve other problems that arose while you were solving the first problem. You have to do it at home, work, school, church, and even while you are driving, walking, or simply sitting on your sofa. Life is problematic. Get used to it.

But while you're getting used to it, learn to manage these problems better so they don't frustrate you and cause you to miss the more important moments of your life or, worse yet, life itself. Jesus said, "Each day has enough trouble of its own" (Matthew 6:34, NIV).

Therefore, according to the Son of God, every day of your life will be filled with distractions that flow from mere survival and from the things you do simply to keep the machinery of your life running. So if you tend to fall into the trap of letting little distractions consume your time and your mental energy, you are walking in dangerous territory. Be careful to avoid the tendency of allowing life's little problems to steal the precious time you should be devoting to more worthy things.

The key is balance. It's okay to get on the telephone when necessary to resolve a disputed claim with your insurance company or to take the time to research the two contractors you are thinking about hiring to repair your leaky roof. You have to do these things to survive in the real world. But if you get in the habit of allowing these kinds of small and insignificant things to totally consume your time or your thinking, you are going to wake up one day and realize that you really didn't do very much with your life.

During your test, therefore, focus on your vision, on your index card. In between all the problems and distractions, take a few breaks just to pull your card out of your pocket so you can remind yourself about what is most important in your life. In fact, if you can discipline yourself to do that, you may very well derive an extra, unexpected benefit from this test. Not only will you discover the connection between your thinking and your destiny; you may also develop the mental discipline to keep the various components of your life in their proper order. You may learn how to handle all your daily problems without allowing them to handle you, deal with the inconveniences of life without letting those inconveniences sap your energy, deplete your joy, or distract you from your relationships and your life's purpose, and control your obligations instead of allowing your obligations to control you.

2) AS MUCH AS POSSIBLE, STAY POSITIVE IN YOUR THINKING.

On an internet website devoted to stories about personal success, one anonymous woman (let's call her Carolyn) shares her story about the ways her negative thinking used to affect her life and how a change in her perspective helped turn her life around.

It seems that Carolyn was a pessimistic sort of person. By her own confession, she was consumed with negative thinking, which dictated her actions most of the time. "More often than not, I used to tell myself how things are not going to happen the way that I want," Carolyn says. Therefore, according to Carolyn, "no" was the North Star of her thinking, the guiding philosophy of her life.

For example, when Carolyn was in college, she would tell herself before every big test that she was going to fail that test. In her mind, regardless of what she did, she was not going to pass her exam. In retrospect, Carolyn actually believed on a subconscious level that a positive attitude about her test would have brought her "bad luck" while a pessimistic attitude would have brought her a little "good luck." In her warped way of thinking, she would be pleasantly surprised by exceeding her expectations, so she set her expectations low. She would have been disappointed if she had set the bar high for herself and had fallen short of those expectations. Subconsciously, Carolyn was learning to "catastrophize," psychologically preparing herself for the failure she was anticipating. Do you see how twisted and destructive this kind of thinking can be in real life?

What Carolyn failed to understand as a young woman was that every negative projection had the effect of lowering her expectations to a point where she was willing to accept behavior in her life that was beneath her potential. On a subconscious level, Carolyn would fail to study adequately for an important exam because she was already convinced that she would not pass the exam, regardless of what she did to prepare for it. If she had been more confident about her abilities, she would have studied harder and scored better on most of her tests. So in hindsight, Carolyn is now convinced that her grade point average in college would have been much higher if she had only known back then what she knows now.

What Carolyn has come to realize is that this type of thinking is not only false; it is self-defeating. It robbed her of a lot of years when she could have done bigger things and been open to opportunities that she ignored because of her sense of pending failure. "So I made a purpose of learning how to change my perception," Carolyn wrote. And that pivotal point in Carolyn's thinking became a pivotal point in her life, a life that is much more productive and gratifying than the life she used to live in the darkness of negativity.

"When setting goals," Carolyn explains, "it is of the utmost importance to have in mind the future, to picture yourself obtaining what you desire. Forget about the past and everything else that you lack or dislike."

So as you focus for the next few weeks on the primary goal you have established for your life, don't think about all the reasons your goal should be unattainable. Don't think about how hard it will be to actually achieve the vision that consumes your heart, the reasons your destiny can't become a reality in your life. Don't talk yourself out of believing you can achieve the goal that is written on your little card. Focus on where you want to go and what you want to become. If you do, something amazing will start to happen to you, I promise. Your dream, like a distant landmark on a foggy day, will gradually start to take shape, become more defined as you get closer to it and as the fog begins to lift. In time, you will start to see ways to get over the hurdles that lie between you and your ambitions, to make minor adjustments in your life so the initial aspects of your dream can become tangible. You will begin to see the faint outlines of a road map from where you are to where you want to be, and your whole world can change in a matter of just four weeks.

Perhaps by now, you can start to see the real purpose of this test. It is designed to help you do something you have never been able to do in the past: force you—compel you—to start thinking about something that has been so "cloudy" that you were not willing to give it any serious mental time. Now, thanks to the small requirement that is being placed on you, you will finally have to stop throughout a typical day and purposely think about something bigger than the task that is in front of you.

As you do this day after day, your mind will start connecting some of the little dots to solutions to the obstacles that lie between you and your goals. As time passes, you will start to see a pathway through the rubble; various steppingstones to your destination will emerge from the ground beneath your feet. You will grow increasingly excited about the prospects of actually making your dream come true as you start seeing a potential passageway emerge that you were never able to see before.

Joseph Clough, a best-selling author and motivational speaker, compares subconscious thinking to a GPS in an automobile. Every time the owner of that automobile gets behind the wheel, he buckles his seat belt with the intention of going somewhere specific. If the driver of the car doesn't know how to get where he wants to go, he enters the "coordinates" into his GPS which is designed to direct him every step of the way toward the destination.

But think about this: A person entering information into a GPS always enters the coordinates of the destination he wants to *reach*; he never enters the coordinates of all the places he wants to *avoid*. We should do the same, Clough explains. A person who wants to arrive at a specific destination in life should always "type in" the destination he or she wants to reach and should then travel to that destination one milestone at a time. Oh, and the driver should keep his eyes on the road ahead of him, not the road behind him. He should focus on all those little mile markers that appear in front of him along the way instead of all the bumps and sharp curves he has already navigated.

That way, he can stay on track and reassure himself that the coordinates he entered are actually correct.

The test you will be taking is your first experience with coordinates for your future. It is your "test drive" with a GPS for personal success. It is an inducement for new thinking, a stimulus for new patterns of thought you haven't been able to create on your own.

Typically, when we think about inducement, we think about a situation that is painful or at least difficult: an induced coma or induced labor prior to childbirth. But this is a completely positive type of inducement. Forcing your mind to think a few times each day about something you are not prone to think about is a way of teaching your mind to create images it is not accustomed to creating and to see possibilities it has never seen before. Once the juices start flowing, the creative parts of your mind will come to life and take over from there. The seed that you sow will sprout and become self-sufficient, then fully fruitful. And the possibilities you hatch in your mind will start to excite you and change the way you go about your life. John Maxwell calls it "thinking for a change."

3) LET YOUR IMAGINATION TAKE FLIGHT.

This doesn't mean that you need to start living in the land of make-believe because make-believe thinking won't work in the real world. But at the same time, you cannot do what you cannot imagine. The people who do great and lofty things are the people who imagined those great things before they attempted to do them. So you need to imagine what you want to be, where you want to go, what you want to become, and what you want to do with your limited time in this world. The more you think about these ideals, the more quickly they will morph from mere mental images into real possibilities. The more you ponder them, the more you will conceive additional ideas that can help you piece together a strategy for achieving what you want to achieve with your life. The more you imagine the things you want to do, the more quickly you will find yourself mapping out the initial steps on your road to ultimate success. So let me show you how the right kind of imagination works.

In 1995, a computer programmer had an idea that he thought might be useful. Like most Americans, Pierre Omidyar had lots of stuff he wanted to get rid of, and he knew a lot of other people who had the same problem. Omidyar thought it might be a good idea to give people a way to sell their unwanted items instead of just throwing them away. That's when he came up with a really creative idea. Since he knew how to build websites and he already had a website where he was publishing information about the Ebola virus, Omidyar decided to build an extra page for his site that he could dedicate to selling unwanted personal items. The first item he sold on his new web page was a broken laser pointer.

But the idea caught on, and soon Omidyar found it necessary to create a totally separate website for the new service he was providing. To cover his costs and to make a small profit, Omidyar charged a minor fee for the privilege of selling items on his site, and he called his new venture AuctionWeb. It didn't take long, however, before all those minor fees started adding up, and Omidyar used the profits to expand his site and improve the services he was offering to buyers and sellers. As the profits continued to roll in, Omidyar's pioneer website became more profitable than his full-time job. Just nine months after launching AuctionWeb, Omidyar left his job at General Magic and devoted himself fully to his new venture, which he incorporated in order to streamline his operations.

Today, that website is known as eBay, and eBay is a classic example of what I am trying to share with you here. In today's world, we take eBay for granted. In fact, the basic idea behind eBay could be considered outdated in today's computerized world. But as simple as the concept of eBay was when it was started, nobody ever had that idea until Pierre Omidyar came up with the creative, realistic solution to an ordinary problem. That is the idea behind creativity—behind imagination.

Most great ideas are really no-brainers if you pause to think about them. They make perfect sense, and you wonder why nobody thought about those ideas years before. But until somebody actually came up with those ideas and worked to implement them, the results never existed. We humans take almost everything around us for granted because most things in our everyday lives are so familiar to us. But there are lots of people alive today who can remember a world without those everyday things. There are lots of people who can remember a world without convenience stores, drive-through food service, ATM machines, fast food, and without cell phones, fax machines, or personal computers. For crying out loud, I still have an old belt that has a deep dent in it where I used to hook my pager.

||||||||||||||||||||||||||||||||||||||||||||||||||||||||||||||

MOST GREAT IDEAS ARE REALLY NO-BRAINERS IF YOU PAUSE TO THINK ABOUT THEM.

It's not that all these new things were difficult to create or expensive to build. It's just that nobody had thought of them before. The products and services that we take for granted today didn't exist in the past because nobody had thought of them yet. As soon as somebody thought of them and then mustered the courage to do what was necessary to bring them to life, those gadgets and services became fixtures in our everyday lives. Imagination gave rise to every familiar thing in our world, even those things that we take for granted. And while we drive by these things each day without even noticing them anymore, the people who imagined and built them are not driving to work. Those people are sipping lemonade beside their swimming pools in Beverly Hills.

Sometimes it just takes the tiniest idea to spark one's imagination. Every person experiences one of these "sparks" from time to time. The key is to embrace your ideas instead of dismissing them; act upon them instead of quickly forgetting about them.

Howard Shultz was the general manager of a Swedish company called Hammarplast. With a staff of just twenty people, Shultz directed the United States operations for this foreign business, which manufactured drip coffee makers. Two years into his stint at Hammarplast, Shultz visited a coffee shop in Seattle, curious about all the small orders this coffee shop was placing with his company. The coffee shop was insignificant in the vast world of coffee manufacturing and was not a major client. Nevertheless, Shultz kept in touch with the owners due to their impressive knowledge of coffee. Then one year later, he accepted a job with that same shop as its first-ever director of marketing.

While on a buying trip to Milan, Italy, Schultz noticed something that most other people simply ignored. He noticed that there seemed to be a coffee shop on just about every corner of that well-known Italian city. Not only did these coffee shops serve excellent espresso and a wide variety of coffee-based drinks, they also served as gathering places and meeting venues for the residents of their respective neighborhoods. The Italians in Milan seemed to migrate to these coffee shops to conduct their daily business and to socialize with one another.

So Shultz took his idea back to Seattle, but the owners of the business were not interested in transforming their peaceful little coffee shop into a bustling cafe. Two years later, however, Shultz managed to raise the necessary capital to buy that little coffee shop from his employers, and in 1988 he gave birth to the Starbucks enterprise that all of us know today.

Are you getting the point I am trying to make here, seeing the power of imagination, beginning to grasp the fact that everything we take for granted in our lives—from the movies we watch to the automobiles we drive—did not exist until somebody had the idea of creating them? People who have achieved success through imagination are no better than you—no smarter than you. What has set these people apart and made them so successful is that they have been willing to value their own imaginations, recognize their own creative abilities, and act upon the talents that God gave to them.

I can't tell you how to have an imaginative idea. I just know that about a zillion people have passed through the streets of Milan over the past few decades, and all of these people noticed the coffee shops that were located on the street corners. But not until Howard Shultz came along did anybody have the idea of trying to duplicate that concept in other cities—to replicate that model in the United States, home of the world's largest economy.

In a similar fashion, Phil Robertson turned a simple duck call into a dynasty in Louisiana. Konosuke Matsushita, a twenty-three-year-old apprentice at a Japanese light company, devised a more efficient type of light socket and used that new idea to launch Panasonic, an electronics company that is now worth about $68 billion. Steve Wozniak and Steve Jobs, two college dropouts who worked together developing game software for Atari, established the Apple Corporation. And Walt Disney, perhaps the most successful of all the people we have mentioned here, summarized the power of a simple idea better than anyone else when he said, "I only hope that we don't lose sight of one thing—that it was all started by a mouse."

Where could your idea take you? In 1981, Bonnie McGough, from Caldwell, Idaho, came up with the simple idea for a little invention called the "koozie." You know a koozie when you see one because a koozie is one of those insulated beverage holders that people use to keep canned drinks cold while they are holding them in their hands. Since McGough patented her idea more than thirty-five years ago, people have improved upon her concept and found a lot of new ways to make use of the simple device. (For instance, a koozie is a great tool for advertising.) While I don't know how many people have made money off the koozie, I do know that somebody has made a lot of money. More than likely, a lot of people have made a lot of money from that simple little piece of foam rubber.

So don't be afraid to dream, to imagine. When you were a child, you had no trouble imagining the "impossible" or dreaming about things you wished you could do. Like the one hundred representative people we have been using throughout this book who had dreams of glory when they were children, you, too, had an imagination when you were young that knew no boundaries and honored no restrictions.

But as you grew older, you fell under the hypnotic lure of the siren's song. You fell under the trance that grips most people's minds as they age and lulls them into a sense of complacency where they are quite willing to abandon their dreams, set aside the imaginations that marked their earlier years, and accept mediocrity as their condition in life and "averageness" as their destiny. So whereas you once dreamed of big things for yourself and imagined a life of greatness, now you seem content just to survive from day to day and happy just to have food on the table and a roof over your head.

Start looking at life differently. Go back to some of the purer things that came to you naturally during your childhood. You don't need to surrender to failure or accept mediocrity as a mark of "maturity." Children dream things and imagine things because children have not yet been taught that they aren't supposed to do that because the divine spark of God-likeness that was embedded in them when God gave them life hasn't yet been crushed and choked to death by the negativity of a despairing world.

Jesus (I just can't stop quoting Him!) once said, "Unless you change and become like little children, you will never enter the kingdom of heaven" (Matthew 18:3, NIV). Jesus said this because, although we should never be *childish*, we should always be *childlike* if we hope to attain spiritual excellence or any real success in life because children don't know how to disbelieve. They don't know how to be skeptical, suspicious, unforgiving, unloving, or unimaginative. Children in their natural, unbridled state are the closest reflections of God we will ever see in this world. So never lose your ability to play, dream, or imagine things that are not visible to you at the moment because success is a byproduct of human imagination. If you can imagine it, it could possibly become a reality, but if you can't, it will never become a reality. Everything that has been devised by human hands began as an image in the mind of a "fool" with a strong passion.

If imagination leads to success, how can a person know when she has finally achieved success—crossed over from being average to exceptional, entered the ranks of the 4 percent and left the ranks of the 96 percent? That is the question that requires an answer before you actually start your journey because no man in his right mind would set out on a course without knowing his destination, and no woman with her senses intact would run a race without knowing where the finish line is located.

So here's what you need to know: A person becomes successful as soon as that person knows where he (or she) wants to go and starts taking steps to get there. He is successful at this early stage in his journey because he will never actually arrive at a place where he can stop walking and just stand still, admiring his achievements. Your journey to success will never have an actual conclusion. It will be ongoing, ever-developing and perpetually evolving into newer and better opportunities. The picture of yourself that you see through your imagination today is only a thumbnail sketch of the broader picture you will see tomorrow, and the picture you will see tomorrow will only be a token of the magnificent work of art that will come into focus later in your life. As soon as you reach one mile marker on the journey to where you want to be, another mile marker will become visible on the horizon. Always be striving for the next objective, for greater and greater things as you live out the things today that you envisioned in the past.

It helps to know, therefore, that success isn't a "place." Success is the journey itself, and as soon as you begin, you will be a happy, content and motivated individual with a reason to get up every morning and do the things that are necessary for achieving your end goal. Your vision will consume you, govern the way you use your time, determine the relationships you choose to nurture and dictate the way you choose to spend your money, view the world and instruct your family and closest friends. A vision embraced and activated is equivalent to success in every meaning of that word. A vision doesn't have to be completed for its owner to be successful.

For this reason, don't overly concern yourself about "how" you are going to achieve the goal on your card, especially during this initial test. Believe me, if you are thoroughly convinced that this goal is worthy of your life and you start thinking about it all the time and in positive ways, you won't ever have to think about the "how" part of the equation. The "how" part will come to you in its own sweet time and its own sweet way, but nothing will ever come to you unless you choose to think about it. So if you will put yourself through a brief time of self-discipline in order to teach yourself to think about your dreams consistently, you will naturally start thinking about them without prompting yourself to do so. And remember, what you think about is what you eventually become, what you will inevitably make happen.

I have read a lot of books by a lot of great people who have taught me to think in great ways and strive for great things. But if I were asked to summarize the core content of all those books in just a word or a phrase, I would have to say that success, achievement, greatness, and legacy hinge upon two qualities more than any others: purpose and faith. If a man has a purpose, nothing can restrain him. And if a woman has faith in herself and her pursuits, nothing can hold her back. Purpose and faith give rise to inspiration which is the seedbed of greatness and success.

Nothing worthwhile can ever be achieved without inspiration. It comes from within, out of a person's own heart and mind—a person's imagination. Inspiration is not something a person can learn from others. So although you may have needed inspiration—a steady input of wisdom from others can help bolster your courage and clarify your path as you take the first steps on that journey—you don't need to derive all your inspiration from other people. You can inspire yourself. And with purpose and faith, you can give rise to all the inspiration and imagination you will need to do great things in the world.

"Imagination is more important than knowledge," Albert Einstein once said. "For while knowledge defines all we currently know and understand, imagination points to all we might yet discover and create." So let your imagination flow as you learn to think about things that truly matter, and let your inspiration flow from that imagination until it impacts you and leaves an indelible mark on your soul. Let it shape you, or rather reshape you. And let it set you on a course that will eventually carry you to your legacy and your place of newfound significance. Find a purpose and think about it. And as ideas come to you about how you can achieve the purpose you have imagined, believe in yourself and your own abilities to do what you are thinking about because when all is said and done, you are destined to become what you think. You are destined to be what you imagine.

CHAPTER 8

YOUR HIGHEST POTENTIAL

The price of anything is the amount of life you exchange for it.
—Henry David Thoreau

E arlier in this book, I explained to you the third law of motion as defined by Sir Isaac Newton. According to this principle of physics, whenever one body exerts a force on another body, the second body exerts a reciprocal force on the first body that is equal in magnitude and opposite in direction. In other words, for every action, there is an opposite and equal reaction.

What this means in the context of this discussion is that the outcome of a person's life is the direct result of the things that person has done (or failed to do) over the course of his life. Nobody's life just "happens." Sure, there may be a small number of things outside of us that deeply affect our lives. But the vast majority of the things that happen to us result from the choices we have made, the actions we have taken, the words we have uttered, or the attitudes we have exhibited. They flow from our own actions and choices, not circumstances that are beyond our control. If you really think about it, you will quickly realize that even the external circumstances that affect us are circumstances that we can respond to in ways that we *choose* to respond to them. Consequently, if we could somehow learn to approach life's biggest challenges with a positive mindset instead of a negative one— with wisdom instead of imprudent behavior—even the worst experiences in life could end up contributing to our success.

||||||||||||||||||||||||||||||||||||||||||||||||||||||||||||||

IF YOU REALLY THINK ABOUT IT, YOU WILL QUICKLY REALIZE THAT EVEN THE EXTERNAL CIRCUMSTANCES THAT AFFECT US ARE CIRCUMSTANCES THAT WE CAN RESPOND TO IN WAYS THAT WE *CHOOSE* TO RESPOND TO THEM.

I want to conclude this book with the sobering thought that your life is the product of your own choices, your own actions. You are where you are today because you did things in the past to place yourself there. Every day, you made choices and took actions that led you down a path to a specific place, and you are the one who walked that path. Nobody made you do the things that you did, choose the things you chose. The actions you took in the past were your own and produced an equal and opposite reaction regarding the outcome of your life right now. This is the universal third law of motion.

This is good news, not bad news because it means that if you had the power to shape your life in the past so that it affects the way you live today, then you have the power to shape your life today so you can affect the way you live in the future. You have the power to turn things around and travel in a different direction toward a different destination. Because you had the ability to shape the first part of your life, you have the ability to shape the rest of your life. And the rest of your life can be the best of your life. You just have to start doing things differently. When you do, your life will have a different outcome because for every action there is an opposite and equal reaction, and the actions you take today are guaranteed to produce their assigned reactions tomorrow.

This truth, however, is another one of those harsh realities of life. You will never achieve anything meaningful in life without paying a price for your success. The person who is willing to pay the price today is the person who will enjoy the benefits of those sacrifices tomorrow. The person who is unwilling to make sacrifices today will reap fewer benefits later on.

Have you ever seen an attractive person with a nice figure or an impressive physique that makes you just a little envious? I can promise you that person doesn't sink into a recliner every night to eat potato chips and watch old movies. She eats properly and exercises regularly, gets the proper amount of sleep each night and drinks a lot of water. Nobody over forty gets to look like a teenager without paying a steep price for that blessing.

Likewise, have you ever known a person who is approaching retirement age with a sense of security and financial wellbeing? Then I can promise you that that person refused to spend all his money on toys and leisurely pleasures earlier in his life. He saved, invested and lived beneath his means in order to put money away for his future.

Elon Musk was just twenty-four years old when he co-founded a software company called Zip2. Zip2 did well from the beginning and grew rather quickly, supporting renowned clients like the *New York Times* and the *Chicago Tribune*. So eventually, Musk sold his growing company to Compaq for more than $300 million.

At the age of twenty-eight, Musk was already worth $22 million, his share of the profits from the sale of Zip2. Obviously, therefore, he could have lived in comfort for the rest of his earthly life, but Musk wasn't looking for comfort. Knowing that he had not yet fulfilled the goal statement he had written on his own index card when he was younger, this youthful entrepreneur was just starting on his journey.

With a passion to do more, Musk used $10 million of his proceeds to start another company, x.com, which merged with yet another company to become PayPal. And just three years after the merger, PayPal was sold to eBay for a whopping $1.5 billion, netting Musk somewhere around $175 million. (He was the company's largest shareholder.) So if $22 million wasn't enough for Musk, $175 million would surely be plenty. Right? Especially considering the fact that he was just thirty-one years old at the time.

No, he was still just getting started. Even before PayPal was sold to eBay, Musk had already committed $100 million of his money to a new business he had always wanted to create, SpaceX because Musk's dream wasn't to get rich and sip virgin cocktails on a beach some-where in Costa Rica. Musk's dream was to build things that had the potential of changing the landscape of the universe forever. Quite a mission statement for one young individual! But this was the kind of legacy that drove Elon Musk to take the risks to make the sacrifices that he made. Musk wanted a bigger payoff in the future, a payoff that transcended money.

I don't know what you have heard about SpaceX, but the basic idea behind this innovative company is the opening of space travel and space technology to the business world and the lowering of the costs of space technology. Until the company was started, all space-related programs were reserved for the governments of the world's largest countries. But SpaceX, founded in 2002, is the first privately held entity in the world to successfully launch, orbit, and recover a spacecraft, vertically land a rocket on a ship in the ocean, and send an observation satellite beyond earth orbit. A mission to Mars is now being planned.

SpaceX, though, came within days of bankruptcy. In the beginning, there were lots of setbacks, and the venture was about to go broke when NASA offered the firm a $1.6 billion contract to develop the technology needed to deliver cargo to the International Space Station. Musk was willing to put it all on the line—not to make money, but to fulfill his life's purpose. And he has made tremendous sacrifices in order to place himself in a situation where his dreams can actually come true. Musk is a poster child for the principle of making sacrifices today in order to achieve great things tomorrow.

Musk is also a living example of the principle that a person becomes what he thinks about because a person ends up doing what he thinks about. Over the course of a person's life, actions and decisions accumulate to produce a particular outcome for that person's life. The person whose thoughts motivate him to pay for success today so he can reap the benefits of success tomorrow is virtually guaranteed success down the road. The person who takes action today to ensure her happiness tomorrow will experience an opposite and equal reaction from life in the months and years ahead. Her self-denial right now will result in abundance and prosperity later on.

||||||||||||||||||||||||||||||||||||||||||||||||||||||||||||||||||

THE GREATER THE SACRIFICE, THE GREATER THE REWARD! THE FEWER THE SACRIFICES, THE FEWER THE REWARDS!

In his blog post titled "The Price of Success: What it Actually Takes to Achieve a Goal," Adam Sicinski, founder of IQ Matrix and self-proclaimed "mind mapper," says, "No matter what goals or aspirations you might have, there is one thing certain: There is a price you must pay to get what you want in life. In fact, there is no sidestepping the fact that any type of success demands something from you. It's simply the way life works, and rarely will shortcuts ever get you there." The price of success isn't cheap. The price is sacrifice.

As you ponder this truth, let me warn you about an ever-present danger in this matter. Some people are smart enough, clever enough, and manipulative enough to fool the people around them a lot of the time. In fact, some people are smart enough and charming enough to fool the people around them all of the time. So if you have the rare ability to charm your way into certain places, you might be tempted to think that you can find ways to bypass the third law of motion. Never forget, however, that though you may be slick enough to fool people, you can never fool life, not even part of the time. The laws of nature are firmly established, and they are entrenched and inflexible. Just as the land is programmed to reproduce the seeds that are planted in it, so life is programmed to give you back an equal and opposite dosage of what you have placed into it. Thus, your success will be in direct proportion to the effort you have put forth to achieve that success and the price you have been willing to pay to obtain it.

If you want to be healthy and fit, you might be able to fool Mother Nature for a while simply on the basis of your excellent genetics. Eventually, though, you are going to have to drink more water and less soda, go to bed earlier and party a little less, and eat more vegetables and fewer hamburgers with Thousand Island dressing and mayonnaise. If you want to be a doctor, you might be able to get into college through your father's connections and your own social charm. But eventually, you are going to have to study hard, spend a lot of money on books and tuition, and go into debt to start your own practice.

The point is this: Nothing in life is free. Everything worth having will cost you something. The irony is that gratification today usually extracts a heavy payment tomorrow while self-discipline today usually pays dividends tomorrow. And frankly, most people (about 96 percent) prefer to take the easier path, gratifying their every desire today while hoping that they can somehow defy the laws of nature tomorrow by reaping great benefits without paying the required price. That is why only 4 percent of people succeed while the vast majority fail to achieve the kind of lives they envisioned for themselves when they seized life by the horns and started walking their individual paths toward the future.

So what is the price that a person must pay for success? Understanding that each person's definition of success is different because each person's vision for life is different, what are the sacrifices that a person must be willing to make in order to achieve the things he or she wants to achieve and acquire the things he or she wants to acquire?

1) PEOPLE INTENDING TO CONTROL THEIR LIVES MUST BE WILLING TO CONTROL THEIR THOUGHTS.

Remember, your mind is "central control" for your life, but your mind will only reproduce what you sow into it. If you sow seeds of life, you will reap a harvest of life. If you sow seeds of death, you will reap a harvest of death. If you sow success, you will reap success. If you sow failure or mediocrity or envy or prejudice, you will reap failure, mediocrity, envy, and prejudice in abundance.

You cannot control the reproductive powers of your mind any more than you can control the reproductive powers of the soil. You get to choose the "seeds," and if you are dissatisfied with the seeds you have planted thus far, the good news is that you can start planting some different seeds that will produce a different harvest for you in the future. The choice is yours. You are in control.

The thing to remember above all else is that your life is the direct result of the things you actually do which flow from the things you think about. These flow from the seeds of thought that you allow to germinate in your mind because those seeds of thought eventually give rise to actions, which eventually give rise to consequences. The course of one's life is determined by the gradual accumulation of words and deeds—the products of thoughts and beliefs. You have the power to shape (or reshape) those things.

Take charge of your own life instead of being a victim. Be positive instead of negative. Appreciate instead of complaining. Build people up with your words instead of tearing them down. See the possibilities instead of the improbabilities. Focus instead of being mentally scattered all over the place. Thrive instead of merely surviving. Do all of these by surrounding yourself with people who will help you fill your mind with noble thoughts instead of the commonplace ideas that consume most people every day. In other words, feed your mind with wisdom instead of garbage or meaningless palaver.

The ability to think is the greatest ability you possess. It is the most wonderful talent God ever gave you. The fact that you can reason about things that are happening today, reflect on the past, imagine the future, and contemplate your origins and ultimate destiny is the quality that distinguishes you from all the other animals that inhabit this planet. Because God made you in His image, with the ability to think in the abstract, you have the capacity to imagine things and to contemplate complex philosophical principles, something no other species can come close to doing. That you can think negatively about things is your Achilles heel. That you can regret the past, fear the future, and be unconscious of your own mental abilities is perhaps the biggest curse and challenge you must confront and overcome.

God made you with the capacity to do amazing things, but the principle of sin operating in the human race has inclined you and every other person in the world to use your mental energies to think in destructive ways. Our thoughts, therefore, can either be our best friends or our worst enemies. It is up to us as individuals to determine whether the "good side" or the "dark side" of our minds will prevail. Positive thinking is a choice.

Some researchers estimate that the average person thinks around seventy thousand thoughts per day. That's a lot of thoughts, more than one every second of your life (assuming eight hours of sleep per night). If the majority of those thoughts is unproductive, destructive, or just downright worthless, you won't be able to avoid the power of all that negativity. Your life will be a reflection of the bad thinking that dominates your mind. But to change your thoughts—even a few of them—is to change that scenario because a change in one's thoughts can automatically change one's feelings. When our feelings change, our decisions change, and then our actions follow our decisions.

So who's controlling your thoughts? Are you controlling them, or are they being controlled by conditioned responses to the circumstances around you that you have learned from others over the course of your life?

One of the negative controlling thought processes that we learn from other people is inner criticism. Over the course of our lives, we pick up the negative thoughts and feelings that originate with other people, especially our parents. We pick up unrealistic expectations of life that we create for ourselves or that other people create for us. We pick up the unhealthy practice of comparing ourselves with other people, never knowing the full story of who those people are behind closed doors, what problems they are hiding from our view, or how they actually achieved the things that they achieved in life. In addition, we can be controlled by the untrue things we have told ourselves in the wake of painful or traumatic experiences.

Another controlling agent that can make us think in unhealthy ways is worry. Humans tend to worry about everything all the time. We worry about the future because we cannot control it and the past because we cannot change it. Nothing is more fruitless and self-destructive than worry, yet fear and worry dominate many people's thinking.

Reactionary thinking can control our lives, as well. Human beings are actually great big chemical cocktails. Inside our brains are many different endorphins and other chemicals that bring us pleasure, anger, happiness, and shame. Certain things trigger these chemicals. If a person isn't careful, that person can easily be controlled by something as simple as the smell of someone's perfume. This subconsciously reminds him of an ex-girlfriend, which triggers all kinds of emotions rooted in the past. If your life is directed by the mechanics of your subconscious rather than your deliberate choices, you are not controlling your own thinking.

Then there are the thoughts that can keep us awake at night. You know, the inability to shut down your brain when you are trying to solve a difficult problem, get over the emotions that course through your veins following an argument with your spouse, or clear a piece of unexpected bad news out of your head for the night! As long as these kinds of thoughts are controlling you, you aren't controlling them or your life. You must be willing, therefore, to learn how to replace old thinking with new thinking and to identify and deal with those recurring thoughts that are depleting your mental energy and hindering you from pursuing better things. The first step to changing bad thinking is being able to identify your bad thoughts, so you can finally do something to interrupt them and replace them with positive thoughts.

2) PEOPLE INTENDING TO ACHIEVE THEIR HIGHEST POTENTIALS MUST BE WILLING TO REMOVE ALL LIMITS FROM THEIR MINDS AND ALLOW THEIR MINDS TO SOAR.

Do you remember what I wrote earlier about imagination? Imagination alone won't cause things to be any different in your life. You have to work, sacrifice and strategize a viable plan for making your imaginations come to life. Only then can you hope to transform the mental images of imagination into the tangible achievements of real life. But until you can imagine something, there won't be any hard work or sacrifice to make it happen, any plans to give rise to the things you hope to achieve. Imagination, therefore, is the first step toward achievement, the portal to change, the entryway to all the potential you were created to enjoy.

If you feel like you have failed to achieve your full potential thus far, your limited success is probably not due to a lack of hard work. Instead, you have probably allowed your mind, the seedbed of your destiny, to be restricted in its imagination. You have sown the wrong kinds of information or too much negative information, immersed yourself in routines and environments that have numbed your creativity instead of awakening it. To really do something significant with the rest of your life, you will need to set your mind free from the limitations you have placed on it and start thinking in new ways instead of settling for what you know.

One of the greatest pivot points of your life can be the moment when you finally realize that your limitations are mostly self-imposed. Another can be the moment you realize that those self-imposed limitations are being strengthened by the people who surround you and perpetuated by the environment in which you live. When you awaken to the fact that you were the one who chose your friends because they made you feel comfortable and you were the one who settled for your environment because it was familiar to you, you can begin to grasp the fact that you have the ability to start making better choices that can write a different script for the remainder of your life. You can begin to grasp the power inherent in the fact that you have the ability to build new relationships and to change the environment in which you live or work.

Just think about that for a moment! Do you know someone who grew up in your hometown, but then moved away to another country or to a distant place with a completely different culture from the one you both knew as children? Did the person change due to his or her exposure to new ways of thinking and behaving? Of course! Perhaps some of those changes were positive while others were negative, but you cannot deny that they were real. The person was totally changed in thought and behavior due to the influences of a different environment. In fact, the person you are thinking about right now was probably changed so much by the new environment, he or she really wouldn't fit in any longer if it was suddenly necessary to move back to the town where the two of you grew up.

Personal changes flowing from a change in environment are more than just rare occurrences; they are real. People really do go through significant changes when they move from one place to a totally different place, and these changes are readily observable to anyone who watches the transition that takes place in these people's lives.

Not long ago, I read an article written by Patrick Whalen. On the website Off The Grid News, Whalen's "What City People Must Know Before Moving to the Country" drove home what I am trying to explain here. He gave some practical advice to city dwellers regarding the unexpected changes they might go through if they suddenly decided to move from their urban environments to more rural ones. He explained to the "city folk" reading his article how urban and rural settings mold people in different ways. In his comments, Whalen wrote about the "rules" that shape people differently in each environment and the shock factor that people have to endure in order to transplant themselves from the fast-paced life of the city to the more laid back setting of the country.

For one thing, people in the city live lives that make them pretty much anonymous. They are visible, but nobody really knows them or even notices them. They are there, but nobody cares. This gives them the ability to hide in plain sight. A person living in New York City could be a really strange character in a number of different ways, but as long as he or she doesn't harm other people, nobody in New York will care very much. Not so in the country! In the country, every eye is upon you, and your every move becomes the talk of the town (if an auto parts store and two stoplights can be considered a "town"). In the city, you can blend in without really trying. In the country, everyone within a twenty-mile radius will know you have arrived before you finish unpacking your car.

Another stark difference between urban and rural life that Whalen mentions in his article is the interdependence of people in small towns and the countryside. In the city, if you come home to discover that your toilet is leaking, you simply call the landlord or contact a plumber. In the country, there probably aren't any plumbers close by, so people learn to help themselves. When they can't help themselves, they help one another. In fact, country folk depend on one another for a lot of the things they need in order just to survive. One neighbor helps another neighbor, and, in return, the neighbor receiving the aid gives it back when a reverse situation arises.

Finally, Whalen explains "outsider syndrome." In the city, people rely on the local infrastructure for security and safety. But in the country, trust is the most essential quality for survival. Unfortunately, it takes a little while to build the kind of trust a person will need to thrive in a rural setting. Country people have to get to know someone before they can totally trust that person. City people need to understand this.

I hope you get my point. Our environments shape us, so a change in environment can actually change us. If you don't like certain things about yourself or your thinking, you may want to take a long look at the effects of your environment. If it proves to be a detriment to your future growth and success, you may want to do something to change certain elements of your environment.

You have become the product of the way you think, and your thinking has been shaped by the people and culture you have allowed to shape you. In the same way that a person can literally move to another state or another country where there is a totally different approach to life, you can move in your thinking from your old, familiar paths toward a new way of viewing the world. Most of the time, you can make this move without physically changing your residence. You can rise above the narrow-mindedness, the pettiness, and the silly prejudices and superstitions that have subconsciously controlled you thus far. You can release your mind from its prison, so it can soar as God intended.

3) PEOPLE INTENDING TO SUCCEED MUST BE WILLING TO DISCIPLINE THEMSELVES TO THINK POSITIVELY ABOUT THEIR OWN POTENTIAL AND LIVES.

Do you have certain problems that just seem to hang around, hindering you in your pursuit of success? Do you see mountains looming between you and your goals that just seem too tall to scale? Well, join the club. Life isn't easy, and nobody will ever hand you success on a silver platter. That's why a mere 4 percent of the people out there make the journey from the valley of failure to the pinnacle of triumph. Life is a lot tougher in some ways than we want to believe, and it is certainly tougher than what we were led to believe when we were children, fantasizing about the future. Although the journey is arduous and danger-laden, it is well worth making. You can make it successfully if you will take the right path.

The first few steps of a journey are important. Nobody begins a journey until he or she believes it can be finished. Nobody finishes a journey without the same belief. Therefore, the best way to guarantee your failure in life is by thinking negatively about yourself or your prospects. The best way to give yourself a fighting chance at achieving your goals is to learn to think positively.

In my opinion, the best way to think about your limitations is to not think about them at all; to look beyond your limitations is to actually look over them. In 1492, before Columbus sailed to the New World, all the educated people of his generation thought the world was flat and that the earth was the center of the universe. They thought this because nobody had ever seen the other side of the ocean. Once Columbus traveled there and brought back the artifacts of his adventure, thinking changed and the world changed as a result.

Similarly, the person who stays trapped in limited thinking is incapable of seeing what is beyond the horizon or on the distant shores of lands beyond the sea. That's where personal vision comes into play because a man or a woman with a vision can see beyond the pettiness of the "little" things that surround them and beyond the temporary status of today's problems to catch sight of a greater and grander purpose that awaits them in their New World. It takes courage, however, to think and to act differently than the people around you, just as it took courage for Columbus and his crew to convince King Ferdinand and Queen Isabella of Spain to underwrite their mission. It took courage for them to confront the elements of the sea and the uncertainty of their westward voyage in order to actually pursue the things they claimed to believe.

Just because you now have a vision for your life, that is no guarantee that problems aren't going to arise to impede your journey toward achieving it. Having a vision can keep you focused on your goal though instead of the problems that are there to distract you and to tempt you to lose your strength for the battle. There is no such thing as a problem without a solution. Unfortunately, most people don't think that way, so they allow the inevitable problems that accompany any great endeavor to sap their strength and deplete their courage. They give up before they ever really start. The person who can keep her eyes peeled on the prize will find ways around her problems as she marches determinedly toward her chosen destination. In fact, a person with a vision fixed in her mind can usually think of several possible solutions to each problem that arises on her journey to her destination.

Do you really think that the world's greatest achievers had a joy ride to the places they reached in life? Or that the people who changed the world with their imaginative thinking became successful without facing problems or failure? According to *The Huffington Post* (September 25, 2013):

- Bill Gates's first business was a total failure.

- Albert Einstein could not speak until he was four years old.

- Jim Carrey, the comedian, was once homeless, living out of a van.

- Bethany Hamilton, the professional surfer, lost her left arm in a shark attack and yet came back to win.

- Benjamin Franklin had to drop out of school when he was ten years old because his parents could not afford the tuition.

- Richard Branson, the fourth-richest person in the United Kingdom, has dyslexia.

- Stephen King's first novel was rejected thirty times.

- Oprah Winfrey had a baby at the age of fourteen and lost her baby shortly after he was born.

- Thomas Edison tried and failed more than a thousand times before finally perfecting the light bulb.

- Vincent Van Gogh sold only one painting in his lifetime.

- Franklin Roosevelt was partially paralyzed at the age of thirty-nine.

- Simon Cowell's first record company failed.

- Stephen Spielberg was rejected twice by film schools, so he pursued his career without a college education.

- Abraham Lincoln was defeated in political campaigns a total of eight times before winning the presidency.

I think you get the point: Life is problematic. The difference between the people who end up in the 4-percent column and the people who end up in the 96-percent column is not a matter of ease, hardship, gender, race, or any other external form of measurement; the difference between the people who succeed and the people who fall short of their goals is simply mental. People who do great things with their lives in spite of their circumstances think "bigger" than their circumstances. They see their lives beyond their current challenges; they are driven by deep ambitions more powerful than the problems that confront them.

Academy Award winner Charlize Theron is another example of how a little bit of the right kind of thinking can overcome a whole lot of adversity. Theron, born in South Africa, was raised on a farm not far from Johannesburg. At the impressionable age of fifteen, Theron watched her mother shoot and kill her father, who was drunk and attempting to harm her and her mother.

A year after this tragic event, Theron won a local competition and received a one-year modeling contract, so she moved to Milan, Italy, then to New York City to study dance at the prestigious Joffrey Ballet School. But shortly after entering school, Theron injured her knee, and her dancing career, her chosen path in life, was suddenly ended.

Most people would have folded after watching an event as horrendous as the one Theron was forced to watch when her mother shot her father. The typical person would have given up when the dream for her life was suddenly snatched by an uncontrollable turn of events. Theron just kept working and looking for new opportunities that would match up with her talents and experiences.

Then, at the age of nineteen, Theron flew to Los Angeles on a one-way ticket. While cashing a check at a bank, she ran into a talent agent who helped her get started in acting. Today, at forty-one, Theron is the recipient of the Academy Award, Silver Bear, Golden Globe Award, and Screen Actors Guild Award for Best Actress. In addition, she has received several other awards and nominations for her achievements on the silver screen.

The point is, if you can teach yourself to think positively about your innate talents, optimistically about the opportunities that await you and your ability to pursue them, there really are few circumstances in life that can keep you from reaching your goals. Few challenges can hinder you in the pursuit of your dreams.

When your destination is clearly established and your confidence in your ability to get there is strong, you may still encounter a few obstacles along the way because obstacles seem to exist just to separate the truly committed people from all the halfhearted wannabes in the world. But your self-confidence and faith will spur you to act decisively and to use wisdom and discretion in the way you handle people and situations. Success will be much more likely when you learn to take your mind off the problems you encounter and set your affections instead on the good things that await you. "All things are possible for one who believes" (Mark 9:23, ESV). All things are possible for one who refuses to focus on the bitter parts of life, focusing instead on life's possibilities.

4) PEOPLE INTENDING TO ACHIEVE THEIR DESTINIES MUST BE WILLING TO LIVE LIKE NOBODY ELSE, SO THEY CAN EVENTUALLY LIVE LIKE NOBODY ELSE.

This is a sentiment that is often conveyed by Dave Ramsey, author of *The Total Money Makeover*. Referring to the fact that people should learn to tighten their belts and deny their immediate appetites in order to save for the future, Ramsey says, "If you will live like no one else, later you can live like no one else."

To Ramsey, therefore, the end goal is what's important, and today's sacrifices are merely a down payment on tomorrow's abundance. To be debt-free later in life, prosperous, and financially secure, a person must discipline himself to do a lot of unpleasant things today so the lifestyle he wants can become a reality later on. Consequently, the way to future financial prosperity is always a pathway paved with self-denial, discipline, and frugality. You have to live like nobody else is willing to live early in your life, so you can live like nobody else is capable of living later in your life.

In this regard, it is good to know that income and expenditures are always relative. A person who earns a lot of money also spends a lot of money to maintain her affluent lifestyle while a person who earns less money tends to spend less money to maintain her less affluent lifestyle. So when it comes to the future, every person, regardless of income, has an equal opportunity to improved financial status in life. She has an equal opportunity to turn her available cash into more cash.

|||||||||||||||||||||||||||||||||||||||||||||||||||||||||||||||||||

ALL THINGS ARE POSSIBLE FOR ONE WHO REFUSES TO FOCUS ON THE BITTER PARTS OF LIFE, FOCUSING INSTEAD ON LIFE'S POSSIBILITIES.

Just think about it! A person with a graduate degree and a high-paying job also has a bigger mortgage and more costly professional expenses than most of the rest of us, must pay higher taxes and spend more money to maintain his standard of living. By comparison, a person with a high school diploma who works in a retail department store will certainly earn less money, but that person will also have a smaller mortgage, fewer professional expenses and pay less in taxes and less to maintain a more modest lifestyle. Consequently, if a person can keep his standard of living as low as possible while working to increase his income and if that person can resist the temptation to elevate his standard of living as his income rises, that person can start saving and investing his money at an early age, regardless of his financial status. That sort of action will definitely improve his future.

Most people who fall into the 96 percent are people who try to live a sultan's lifestyle the day they leave their parents' homes. Yes, they are smart, talented people. Yes, they often have college degrees. But from their first day in the workforce, they tend to rent apartments they can barely afford, buy expensive cars with huge monthly payments, eat out several times a week, and live off their Visa cards. They take nice vacations (on credit), wear nice clothes (on credit), and do everything possible to impress their friends and members of the opposite sex (usually on credit).

However, the person who learns early in life to live on less than he or she makes and then starts saving and investing what doesn't get spent (at least 10 percent of all earnings) can retire young and live a truly prosperous lifestyle that the credit bureaus can never take away. This person also can pursue his or her dreams regardless of what they might be, because, by the time middle-age rolls around, that person will have, not only the experience and professional reputation to do whatever is desired with the rest of his or her life, but also a means of support while doing it. Start a business, work less and write a book, travel the world with a camera, or go to Antarctica to study the mating habits of penguins—the possibilities are endless!

But the person who lives constantly above his means will be trapped until he is old, desperately wanting to do something fulfilling with his life, yet feeling stuck in a job that he hates so he can afford to pay the bills that he snatches from his mailbox every afternoon when he pulls his heavily financed car into the driveway of his heavily mortgaged house.

I could literally write a book about this subject. In fact, I *have* written a book about this subject (check out *Paid in Full*). But in the limited space I have here, let me just invite you to do the math for yourself. If a young woman starting work immediately after college could discipline herself to live slightly beneath her means and to save just 10 percent of her income throughout her working life, that young woman could easily become a millionaire in twenty to thirty years, probably less. Then her money would just keep earning more money, which would earn more money on top of that money. Perhaps that's why Albert Einstein said, "Compound interest is the eighth wonder of the world. He who understands it, earns it; he who doesn't, pays it."

With the miracle of compound interest working in this young woman's favor and with her own self-discipline and sense of delayed gratification giving her an advantage over those with a more shortsighted view of life, she will definitely be rich, prosperous, and secure at an early age. Then she can laugh at all the people who thought she was crazy for paying cash for used cars and for buying her work clothes at Goodwill because now she can buy whatever she likes, wherever she likes, and she can do whatever she likes with whomever she likes for the rest of her enviable life, and she can pay cash for every bit of it.

You just have to choose. And if you choose wisely, you will find the courage and the self-discipline to say "no" to yourself today (the single greatest quality of the truly successful) so you can say "yes" to yourself later in life (the single greatest benefit of the truly successful).

Consequently, the message I want to convey to you in the closing statements of *Mindset Matters* is that, when all is said and done, action is essential to success. Obviously, you have to know what you want to do and why you want to do it.

I hope this book has helped to point you in the right direction when it comes to those important questions. Once your destination is determined, your gas tank is filled and your bags are packed and loaded, there comes a moment when you have to place the key in the ignition, close the door, start the engine, put the car in gear, and press the accelerator, because, without action, the greatest plans in the world remain unfulfilled and the noblest motivations prove worthless.

Perhaps General Colin Powell summarized my sentiments better than anyone else when he said, "There are no secrets to success. Success is the result of preparation, hard work, and learning from failure." And he is so right. In fact, in one little sentence, General Powell has encapsulated everything I have explained to you in great detail within this book.

Since the dawn of creation, human beings have been looking for a shortcut to success. They have been seeking the hidden trail to the promised land. They have noticed that some of the most unlikely people seem to reach their goals while some of the most "worthy" fall short of theirs. People have always wondered what makes about 4 percent of the population successful while about 96 percent fall short of their goals to one degree or another.

Now you know that there are no "secrets" to a meaningful and fulfilling life—no "hidden paths." Because life is unpredictable, a few lucky souls will always "happen" upon success. They will win the lottery or strike oil in their backyards. But the vast majority of the people who climb to the mountain peak that most of us can only admire from sea level possess a driving motivation in their hearts that gives them direction along the way. With that internal vision guiding them consciously and subconsciously through daily life, they do what they need to do to prepare for their journey. Then they work hard to get where they want to go. Because they are focused, they avoid the pitfalls, distractions, and detours that tend to entrap most of the rest of us. Because they are determined, they don't abandon their ambitions when the car runs out of gas or a tire goes flat on the highway. They learn from their failures, whether those failures were self-imposed or inflicted upon them by circumstances, are extremely careful about the people they invite to sit in the back seat while they make their way to their destination, and bring along with them those people who can help them and encourage them, not distract them or dissuade them.

So let me encourage you to act on the things you have discovered here, to take some initial steps to implement the thoughts you have entertained as you have read through this book. Within you lie the talents and potential to do everything you were created to do and to be everything you were created to be. But until you understand why you have not yet achieved your life's goals and until you actually do something to move the ball forward, nothing in your life will change. It will only get worse because the guilt and regret will increase over time if you fail to act on the newfound knowledge you have acquired.

If you will begin to take some baby steps by teaching yourself to think like the 4 percent who succeed in life and by immersing yourself in situations and cultures that can help you think in a new way, I promise you that your life will begin to change and the course of your life will start to bend in a different direction.

So go for it. The price of success may be hefty, but the price of failure is much higher. May you find happiness, satisfaction, and peace with yourself and others as you make your mark upon the world and leave a lasting legacy for those you love. Learning that your mindset matters may be the best-kept "secret" of the world's most successful people, but the best-kept secret in life is really no secret at all.

||||||||||||||||||||||||||||||||||||||||||||||||||||||||||||||||||||

THE PRICE OF SUCCESS MAY BE HEFTY, BUT THE PRICE OF FAILURE IS MUCH HIGHER.